Elements

of

Providence

during the

Genesis Flood

by; Ben Tripp M.A. Sc., P. Eng.

Elements of Providence during the Genesis Flood

By Ben Tripp M. A. Sc., P. Eng.
Illustrations by Carolyn Tripp B.A.

Other books by the same author:
1. The Window of Life
   A Theory of the Earth based on Asteroid Impact
2. Fairytales for Adults
   Theories of the Earth in Disarray
3. Concerning the Birth of Christ
   A Discussion of the timing of Christ's Birth
4. The Asteroid Theory of the Flood and the Ice Age
   The Necessity and Sufficiency of an asteroid shower to cause an Ice Age
5. Time is Running Out
   The Earth is quite young and time is running out!
6. The Impossibility of Extra-Terrestrial Life
   Could a duplicate Solar System exist?
7.. The non-Myths of the Bible
   Neither the Great Genesis Flood nor Recent Creation are myth.
8. Climate Change and Holy Writ
   An end-time situation in Nature is compared to end time scenarios in Scripture
9. Too Much Carbon
   The Declaration that we must reduce carbon emissions is false

Ben earned Bachelors and Masters of Applied Science degrees in Engineering from the University of Waterloo, Ontario, and has worked as a consulting engineer on such projects as controls for large telescopes and test equipment for the CanadArm. He holds patents for innovations involving the recycling of used tires into fence boards and a novel ground coil arrangement for geothermal heat pumps.

Ben's interest in the current topic, and his related background reading and research span several decades and have culminated in what he purports to be a credible, cohesive and insightful discussion of one aspect of the Great Genesis Flood.

It is his hope that these observations and opinions will be helpful to others in their own investigations.

Registered copyright 2014 by Ben Tripp

This book may not be copied in whole or in part with the exception of brief quotations for reference purposes. While the book is copyright the illustration on page 21, The Galactic Habitable Zone, is independently copyright and cannot be reproduced in any form whatsoever without specific written permission from the author. The author has made serious attempts to recover permission to quote others. Any discrepancies will be addressed immediately. For all other matters relating to copyright please contact the author. Ben Tripp, 24175 Erin/E. Gary T.L., East Garafraxa ON, Canada, L9W 7H1

Tripp, Ben, 2014
Elements of Providence during the Genesis Flood

A bibliography has been included in the appendix. Also an index of key words included at the end of the book enables particular discussions to be found quickly.

Acknowledgements;

Wendy Speziali, formatting
Carolyn Tripp B. A. illustrations

ISBN 978-0-9936349-3-2 Soft cover version
ISBN 978-0-9936349-4-9 Electronic version

This work is dedicated to my family

To my dear wife:
Judith Anne
The love of my life

To my children:
Bryan, Rebecca, Daniel and Carolyn
The great blessing of my life

To my dear grandchildren:
Evelyn, Ayla, Zoe, Izzy and Ben

And to my bonus child:
Andrea

May this humble epistle assist them in their search for truth.

Table of Contents

Table of Contents vii
Foreword ix
1. Introduction 1
2. Ark Survival 3
    2.1   Water movement 3
          2.1.1   Wave Size 3
          2.1.2   Bending Stress 4
          2.1.3   Examples of Stress-Induced Failure 4
          2.1.4   Types of Water movement 6
          2.1.5   Water Burden during the Flood 9
    2.2   Temperature and Light 10
    2.3   Contaminated Air 11
    2.4   Preservation of Hull Integrity 12
3. Temperature Stability 13
    3.1   Temperature Regulation Factors 13
          3.1.1   Heat from the Sun 14
          3.1.2   The Greenhouse Gases 15
    3.2   Results of Temperature Change 16
    3.3   Temperature Regulation Disruption 18
4. The Ice Age 21
    4.1   Popular Ice Age Theories 21
    4.2   Actual Ice Age Requirements 21
    4.3   Rarity of Ice Age Conditions 23
    4.4   Solar Energy Blockage 23
    4.5   The Cold Factors 24
    4.6   The Heat Factors 25
    4.7   The Provision of Temperature Stability 26
5. Orbital Change 27
    5.1   Impulse Transmission 27
    5.2   Asteroid Shower on the Earth 31
    5.3   Asteroid Shower on the Moon 32
    5.4   Other planets 34
          5.4.1   Mercury 34
          5.4.2   Mars 35
    5.5   Aggregate Impulse 35
    5.6   Goldilock's Orbit 36
    5.7   Provision of Temperature Stability 39

6. The Greenhouse Gases 41
      6.1   Pre-impact World c/w Vapour Canopy 42
      6.2   Impact Period 46
      6.3   Ice Age Period 49
      6.4   Climate Transition Period 49
      6.5   Present Climate Period 52
      6.6   Tranquility to Chaos to Tranquility 56
      6.7   Provision of Hot-Cold Balance 58
7. Beringia, an Ice Age Fairy Tale 59
8. Review 61
9. Summary 67
Bibliography 69
Index i

Foreword

In Christian literature the Great Genesis Flood and the Ice Age are closely associated with the two calamities understood to be part of the same overall event. This is in agreement with Scripture as there is only one event reported in the Bible that involved the entire world causing untold agony for all of its inhabitants. Concerning that event it is clearly stated that all land-based animals died. It goes without saying that it would have taken a very unusual and totally disrupting catastrophe to have killed all of the land-based animals. In fact the only ones to escape were reportedly saved by direct involvement of the Deity.

While the report has been identified as religious and therefore slightly less than trustworthy it must also be noted that in spite of several world-wide disasters recognized by the scientific community, there is a great vacancy regarding any survival explanations. In fact the only survival explanation offered by anybody (apart from the Genesis account) is included in the Epic of Gilgamesh (another ancient document) where it also mentions the use of a boat as the means of salvation. Scientific literature is completely void of any discussion of survival and this is curious. While science also claims that several world-wide disasters have occurred, no commentator has become brave enough to offer any discussion of survival. One would think that at least some discussion would have been offered by now. At the same time that certain secular authors have tried to discredit the Genesis account they have stopped short of offering anything themselves. An even sadder corollary is that some Christian authors have made serious attempts to diminish the importance of the Genesis account by claiming that it was really only a local event and did not involve the entire world at all. This is unfortunate because even a cursory reading of the Genesis report makes the world-wide nature of the event completely obvious. Such false interpretations are basically the same as trying to rewrite the Bible and it is sad to recognize that others have done this over the years as well. This should not be done! Besides being arrogant it totally ignores the overwhelming evidence from nature that corroborates the Genesis account completely. The evidence is so blatant that one does not need to be a scientist or any other particular type of specialist to recognize it.

The discussion to follow will be dealing with some of this evidence as well as suggesting aspects of the whole affair that are a little too coincidentally in our favour to have just happened. One is prompted to ask if the arrangement of all of these factors just coincidental. After all, there are a large number of stars and planets in the universe and we might be tempted to think that sooner or later the right circumstances would show up. Such thinking could well be applied to the Earth until we realize that the Earth seems to have been a most favourable place to live prior to a major upset and it obviously is once again a favourable place to be after everything has settled down. There is something unusual and difficult to explain about this!

The host of parameters which must be arranged in very particular ways in order for life to exist on a quiet day on Earth boggle the imagination. In the companion work entitled, The Window of Life, A Theory of the Earth Based on Asteroid Impact, these parameters are referred to as 'windows'. Even as a window has two sides our life-enabling parameters, such as temperature, cannot drift very far in either direction. How would all of these factors have been maintained when the Earth was undergoing such trauma that all land-based animals died? The trauma was so severe that it is hard to describe. While a discussion has been offered in The Window of Life, Part 2, it was never-the-less almost impossible to capture the magnitude of the destructiveness of the event. Even at the present time when the Earth is not being tortured, it is difficult to see how all of our life-support factors can stay lined up indefinitely. In fact, the minor shifts that are currently taking place make many of us shudder because it is very well understood that we need all of our life support factors to remain constant and not deviate into the danger regions. As an example the average world-wide surface temperature of the Earth is about +15C but there is great concern that it might rise to +17C. Two degrees is not really very much but the alarm bells are ringing indicating that at least a significant number of scientists are concerned. This very minor temperature shift makes us wonder how the Earth could have had optimally-favourable-to-life circumstances before a major world-wide calamity and once again have optimally-favourable-to-life circumstances after it was all over? Is this just coincidental? Was the Deity involved in this?

While the Bible is quite clear that there was only one major world-wide calamity, nature is also clear that this was the case as well. There are several lines of evidence to support this in nature and a few of them are discussed herein.

All of the mountain ranges of the world are formed from sedimentary rock. The material for this rock has been deposited by water which would have required unthinkably-massive water flows far beyond anything we experience today. It isn't uncommon for the sedimentary layers to be one thousand feet thick and many are much thicker. What type of water flow would have been required to place this much material in one pass. Such water movement would have poured right over any continent and hardly have slowed down. This would have been very unusual activity and the magnitude of it means that more than one continent must have been involved. It absolutely must have been a world-wide event. Such massive water flows would never have stopped at the boundaries of a single continent but would have carried on for thousands of miles. It would have been a most horrific event!

Further evidence for the singularity of the event comes from an understanding of the consequences that the Earth would experience if only a single large asteroid came in. The popular notion at the present time is that the asteroids that have hit the Earth came at widely-spaced times. That did not happen. They came as a shower, caused unspeakable mayhem and then stopped coming. If a single large asteroid should strike the Earth, all of the calamities outlined below and discussed in much more detail in the companion volume, would have happened. The key that points to a multiple-impact event involves the greenhouse gases. The small portion of the atmosphere that constitutes the greenhouse gas inventory regulates the surface temperature of the Earth and keeps it right where we need it to be kept. If a single large asteroid hit the Earth it would produce a world-wide chill because of the massive dust cloud that would form. The chill would cause a loss of atmospheric water vapour which is our most influential greenhouse gas. Without an adequate level of water vapour in the atmosphere the temperature of the Earth would drop. However the amount of water vapour in the air is solely determined by temperature. Therefore chilling caused by any reason whatsoever would result in a loss of water vapour and more chilling. The only end to this viscous cycle would occur when further chilling did not result in any further reduction in the amount of water vapour in the air. Unfortunately, this would not happen until the temperature was well below freezing. Plainly speaking, if a single large asteroid hit the Earth, it would simply freeze up and stay frozen. All animal life would terminate. The only way that this could be prevented from happening is if other effects of the asteroid impact released enough heat to offset the chill. This is doubtful for a single hit. It would have required an asteroid shower to disturb the crust of the Earth enough to release enough heat to offset the chill produced by the world-enveloping cloud resulting from the impact. While a single large asteroid would produce the cloud and hence the chill, a shower of asteroids would only do the same thing. Once solar energy was kept from reaching the surface, the Earth would chill but more cloud would not be able to intercept more energy because the energy would already have been intercepted. On the other side of the coin, while a single large asteroid would fracture the crust of the Earth thereby causing internal heat to be released, it wouldn't likely fracture it enough to effectively offset the chill. However a shower of asteroids would fracture the crust extensively thereby releasing enough offsetting heat to prevent the Earth from shutting down. The necessary balance of heat and cold so necessary to enable the greenhouse gas inventory to be properly retained (or at least to have the factors in place to enable it to be re-established) would have been produced by a shower but not by a single hit. It is therefore concluded that an asteroid shower occurred and not a single large hit. It is also clear that such a scenario is in complete agreement with the Holy Scriptures.

There is another major problem accompanying the single one-at-a-time-hit hypothesis. Any major hit would be most devastating to animal life. It has often been declared that there would only be a five percent survival from a major hit. Then in few million years there would be another major hit and only five percent would survive that hit as well. Neither would it be five percent of every species. Many species would be completely wiped out altogether. (By the way, the five percent figure is never discussed and never explained.) All of this means that the surviving cohort from each hit would be the starting point for the next period of time. Evolution would really need to work overtime to produce a diversity of creatures before the next devastation. How could this have happened? It also means that the surviving cohort from the last major hit was the starting point for the species diversity that we have at present. Further, this is a time when numerous different species have been lost due to habitat destruction or over-killing. How many different species did the Earth enjoy five thousand years ago? It is also a fact that rats and other vermin would have had a better chance of survival than pigs or horses or deer. Large animals would have suffered the most. Rats are hard to kill. Did the present cohort of animals on the Earth evolve from rats?

The evidence from nature therefore points to a single period of unthinkable devastation. An asteroid shower would have done this and this makes it clear that nature is in complete agreement with the Holy Book.

1. Introduction

The Bible report of the Genesis Flood clearly and obviously contains elements of Providence. There are several components of the report which have no possibility of being understood from a scientific viewpoint. One example is the gathering of the animals. There is no conceivable way that Noah could have rounded up all of the animals and kept them under any semblance of control on his own. There were apex predators and animals that would not have stood a chance of survival in the presence of their most fearsome enemies under any other conditions. There they were side by side with other creatures both large and small and all proceeding in an orderly and timely manner into the Ark. Also they all knew where to go. The staff on hand included only eight people. Such a small crew could not have physically managed so many creatures in any other setting. How do you get a rhinoceros (even if it is just a baby) to go where you want it to go and remain there without bothering anything else? It simply would not be possible even if it was drugged somehow and partially put to sleep. Then after getting on board the entire group had to settle down and basically go to sleep. Movement would have been severely restricted. No exercise would be allowed. Noah and his family would have had enough demands on their time just looking after themselves. It was to be a one-year cruise. Every creature had to stay put. Keeping so many creatures supplied with food and water under any other circumstance would not have been possible by such a small crew. Something else was taking place and Noah and the others were not labouring 24/7 to distribute food.

The timing of the entire affair is also a mystery. While the warning of the coming disaster was given about one hundred and twenty years ahead of time (i.e. 'His days shall be 120 years. Gen 6: 3) it would otherwise not have been detectable by Noah and he would not have had time to prepare for it.

Therefore, even a hasty reading of the Genesis account of the Great Flood event will reveal that there were several aspects of that event which can only be identified as miraculous. These we can refer to as being explicitly Providential. No one could miss them as such. Basically the entire report carries this tone as Noah, the chief character, is reported as talking directly with the Deity. This is most unusual. People do not meet with and discuss anything directly with the Deity. If such a thing ever happened it would properly be identified as miraculous. Neither should anybody wish for such an event. It would be incumbent on any reporter to be very hesitant to jump to such a conclusion. If this were not the case, almost any scenario could be invented and rational explanations would not be necessary.

'The Lord did it and that's all there is to it. So everybody should believe my report because the Lord told me'. We should always be hesitant to accept any such report because activity such as talking directly with God would expectedly be very rare. So rare that centuries could pass before something like this would happen again. In reality not very many of us will ever have a 'hot line to God'. And we probably should not have one because such interaction would carry awesome responsibility. The text however is clear that Noah talked with God so we properly identify such an event as miraculous.

Beside the conversation between Noah and the Lord there are several of the other aspects of the event that are also properly seen as being the direct result of interaction of the Deity. In these other cases the workings of nature have been arranged to bring about a result which would not otherwise have been possible. The gathering and management of the animals is has been mentioned. Then, when it was time to leave the ark, things would not have suddenly changed. All of the creatures had to leave by the same door. How would this have been possible? Those near the door would have to leave first in an orderly manner not unlike vehicles leaving a ferry at the end of a lake crossing. Everybody cannot leave at once.

There are other aspects of the report involving characteristics of our physical world which can be understood from a scientific viewpoint to a certain degree but are so unlikely to be in the correct arrangement that one has to marvel how it could have happened at all. Clearly the Supernatural was involved throughout the entire affair and all aspects of this involvement would properly be termed miraculous. It was not only miraculous, it was obviously miraculous. Science is science but sometimes more than rational evidence-supported developments were involved during the Great Flood Event. When this happens, it is appropriate to recognize it. In so doing the event becomes even more awesome and the merciful nature of God becomes even more evident.

The Great Flood Event was an unimaginable upset for the entire World. The trauma was so intense that all land animals that were not in the Ark died. Further it is almost beyond imaging how anything could survive such a total disaster even if it was on the Ark. As the matter is investigated in more depth several aspects of the happening raise the suspicion that the Deity was much more involved than one might at first suspect. Several of these more subtle factors are the subject of the following discussion.

2. Ark Survival

The survival of the Ark was paramount. There wasn't any back-up plan. It had to get through the catastrophe intact. After that it was an expendable item. It would never float again and would never again be needed. On the other hand perhaps it never could have floated again. During the months that it floated it would have been stressed and would have taken considerable abuse. Therefore reusing it at a later time would probably have been out of the question but since it would never again be needed, that point is moot.

2.1 Water movement

The abuse that the Ark would have suffered would have been caused by water movement. If the water had just been sitting still, the Ark could have just floated quietly until it was no longer needed. Unfortunately for this particular possibility the entire text is full of action verbs. The water was indeed moving and it was moving in a most violent matter. While the Genesis text indicates movement, all of the indicators from the scientific aspect also indicate movement. It would have taken movement to get marine fossils to the top of Mount Everest. It would have taken movement to place the sedimentary layers that form all of the mountain ranges of the world and it would have taken movement to place whale remains high on Antarctica as well as in the interior of North America – including Ontario. The water was moving and it was moving violently.

2.1.1 Wave Size

The Ark was, by any consideration, a large vessel. In fact it was the largest boat ever built right up to the time of the Great Eastern in the mid-eighteen hundreds. There is a good reason that large boats were not built until more recently. It is simply because they would not have been strong enough. In this case strength is required to withstand the bending applied to every large boat on the ocean.

When the wind blows across the water, waves form. These waves get bigger the further and faster the wind blows. On the ocean, the wind can blow for hundreds of miles without being interrupted. This means that ocean waves can become quite large. As they get larger the breaking-over-the-top factor becomes a lesser feature of the wave when compared to the actual wave size. When a wave becomes very large it is sometimes called a roller. Rollers can have vertical heights of 40 or 50 feet and wavelengths of several hundred feet. The long wavelengths (i.e. the distance from one wave top to the next one) also mean that the wave will be moving fast.

The relationship between wave length and wave speed is well understood by sailboat designers so much so that longer boats are intentionally built just to get more speed. There is a relationship between the length of a boat and its speed for displacement-hull boats. In order to avoid this limitation a different type of hull must be used called a planing hull. With a planing hull and enough power a boat can ride right up on top of the wave that it forms due to its forward movement and in fact overcome any other waves that come into its way. To do this does require a lot of power and neither very large boats nor sailboats have such power so their speed has historically been limited.

2.1.2 Bending Stress

A large boat becomes severely stressed when its length closely matches the distance from the peak of one large wave to the peak of the next one. Minimal stress is applied to a large boat if it simply sits in calm water. In this case, the water supports the boat along its entire length. However when the average wavelength of a train of waves matches the boat length, the boat is alternately supported at its ends and in the middle. Alternating the support of the boat in this way causes the boat to bend up and down at the middle. If it is not strong enough to withstand such repeated bending, it will break. In fact the problem develops long before the worse-case scenario is reached with the wavelength matching the boat length. If a boat is supported by a wave at its middle and the next wave peak is slightly to the rear of the stern, the stern will not be supported properly. At the same time if the preceding wave was slightly ahead of the bow, the bow will not be supported properly either. In a case like this the wavelengths involved would be slightly greater than one-half of the length of the boat. Wavelengths of this size and longer would be serious trouble for any large ship which was not designed to withstand the stresses that they would cause. Naval history includes several examples of this type of situation where the boat could not stand the stress and simply broke at the middle and sank.

2.1.3 Examples of Stress-Induced Failure

The Edmond Fitzgerald was a large lake freighter designed to carry ore on the Great Lakes. It was a long ship as are many of the freighters travelling on the Great Lakes. In fact it would have been built to the maximum length that could get through the locks at Sault Saint Marie.

On its fateful journey it left Thunder Bay to travel across Lake Superior to Sault Saint Marie with a full load of ore. Almost as soon as it left port a storm blew up from the north-west. This would have caused the waves to develop in almost exactly the same direction as the ship was moving. This is called a following sea and the waves coming down the lake would have been following and overtaking the Edmond Fitzgerald. In fact, they were following it to its doom.

The further waves travel with the wind, the larger they get. As on the ocean, waves get bigger and bigger until rollers are formed. These rollers move quickly because the speed of a water wave is directly related to its length. Lake Superior is a large lake and as such, waves occasionally develop that are similar to ocean waves. In this case the wind was blowing down the lake in the exact direction to enable waves of maximum size to develop. This means that as the south-east end of the lake was approached, the waves would have been reaching their maximum size. This would not be good news for any large ship and certainly was not good news for the Edmond Fitzgerald because it sank at the south-east end of the lake.

How fast and how long would the waves have had to have been to threaten the Edmund Fitzgerald? The boat was about 730 feet long. This means that if a series of roller waves crested at or longer than 400 feet from peak to peak, the hull of the Edmond Fitzgerald would have been very badly stressed. A wave of this length would have had a speed of about 30 mph. Of course waves never form perfect wave trains and randomness is always involved. However if such wave speeds (or even less when randomness is considered) had developed during that storm, the survival of the boat would have been threatened.

The remains of the boat were found on the bottom of Lake Superior at the eastern end and broken in two with the two pieces completely separated. The front half was up-right. The back half was upside down. Unfortunately the official explanation of the break-up did not acknowledge the wave-induced stress factor at all. It put the blame on water splashing past the hatch covers and into the hold from crashing waves. With this explanation the water would have had to enter the hold from the top through the hatch covers. This explanation therefore demands that two things were happening. First, the hatch covers were leaking and second, waves were repeatedly breaking over the deck. Both of these factors are dubious. While some of the hatch covers were found to be missing, all of the clamps were in excellent condition. If the hatch covers had been missing the crew would have noticed and taken corrective action. The crashing-waves question is also dubious. It was a following sea and the waves would have been approaching the ship from the rear. If they were indeed traveling at about 30 mph (i.e. slightly faster than modern boats) and if the ship was moving forward at possibly one half of that speed, the waves were hitting the rear of the boat at about 15 mph. However there weren't any hatch covers at the rear of the boat but rather a large superstructure which would have blocked waves from even reaching the deck at all!

The official explanation recognizes that the ship broke in two but declares that this happened when it hit the bottom of the lake. However one piece of the boat was found upside down and the other piece was upright. It is also known that a particularly large wave passed just before it sank. The more realistic explanation is that it broke apart at the surface due to the stress caused by large, passing, roller-waves. The cargo would have spilled from the opening causing it to open further. Then the two parts could have sunk independently to the bottom. If the boat had simply become over-loaded with leakage water and then sank there is no good reason to think that it would completely break in two at the bottom. If it had fractured on landing we would expect that the two parts would have still been at least partially attached and basically in the same orientation and attitude.

Lake freighters are very long boats and not designed to accommodate the stresses caused by ocean rollers. That is one reason that lake freighters do not travel on the ocean. Any boat intended to be operated on the ocean must be designed to accommodate the stresses that a heaving sea can generate.

A second example of a ship breaking in two is the Titanic which sank in the Atlantic Ocean early in the 20th century. This sinking was well witnessed as many people escaped from the sinking ship in life boats and stood by while it sank. In this case the ship could not withstand the stress that built up as the front end, which became filled with water that had entered through a large iceberg-caused rip in the side, sank. As it sank the back end was raised right out of the water. This means that the back end was not supported by the water and very great stress developed in the steel through the midsection. The steel used at that time was not nearly as strong as steel used today and the large steel plates were held together with rivets. Rivets are not used for this purpose any more. Modern ships are built using very strong steel with the separate plates being held together by full-depth welds. The welds are as strong as the steel. The net result is that ships are very strong in comparison to a century ago and they are properly designed for every imaginable stress that might be encountered.

Very large long boats cannot travel on the ocean without being built to recognize the types of waves that could readily develop on any ocean crossing.

A further example of a type of boat that would never be taken out on the ocean is the river boats of Europe. These boats are very long in comparison to their height and would not even fair well on a large lake as soon as the distance between wave peaks was slightly greater than one-half of their length. In this case, since these boats might be 300 feet long, a wave that measured a little more than 150 feet from peak to peak could spell trouble. Such a wave would only be travelling at about 18 mph which is not very fast compared to the wind speeds that can easily develop on a lake during stormy weather.

2.1.4 Types of Water movement

In order for a boat to be capable of traveling on a large body of water it must be capable of carrying the stresses that will develop if the water is not calm and level. During the Great Genesis Flood the water was neither calm nor level. It consisted rather of a continuous series of waves, large and small coming from all directions. (We recall that Genesis 8, verse 3 is usually translated 'continually' whereas an expanded translation of the Hebrew, which is actually a two-part phrase, means 'a going followed by a coming, a coming and going repeatedly') These waves over-ran the land (Genesis 2, verses 18 and 19, 'prevailed exceedingly' and covered 'all the high hills'.) 'Continually' is followed by 'from off the land'. It seems that the waves were rolling right over the land and going off the other side. In order to do this horizontal movement was required. Therefore included in the mayhem was horizontal movement of the water which doesn't happen at all on the lakes and oceans today. The only exception to this is the horizontal sheet-flow that develops when a tsunami comes into shallow water and then runs up onto the land. A recent example of this type of water movement occurred during the Japanese tsunami which happened a few years ago. The forward movement of the water became very evident as the water approached and flowed over the breakwater. The height of the originating tsunami was much lower than the breakwater but due to the kinetic (or moving) energy of the forward movement, the water was able to climb up and roll right over it. Then it continued inland and only stopped when elevated areas were reached which were high enough so that the potential energy at the highest location reached was equal to the kinetic energy of the moving water. If the water had been moving forward faster, it would have been even harder to stop and even higher land forms would have been required.

There is a second reason that many of the waves were mountain climbers and that is because of their height. When an asteroid lands directly on water, it forms a temporary crater in the water. A portion of the water from this crater would be ejected from the area as splash water. This water would soar out across the surrounding area and rain down on everything for miles around. While a portion of the volume of this temporary crater would leave the area as a splash, the remainder would be pushed outward with incredible force. A mountainous ring of water around the crater opening would thereby be formed and it would have been given an outward push. The height of this circular mountain would be commensurate with the size of the asteroid. In the Chesapeake Bay example on the Eastern Seaboard of the USA, the crater is about 50 miles in diameter. Ground material is harder to displace than water so it is safe to assume that the temporary water crater would have been at least this large. Most of the water that was pushed aside to form the crater would have quickly piled up to form the water mountain. To suggest that this mountain would have been several miles high would not be exaggerating in the least. It could have been five miles high. It could have been ten miles high. In any event it would have been a monster. The wave from the Chesapeake Bay impact could explain the presence of marine fossils under Paris, France. A great wave brought these fossils to that location and it could have been the one produced when the Chesapeake Bay asteroid landed. These would have been globe-encircling waves and only a very high mountain could have stopped them. Some impact sites indicate that the asteroids that caused them would have been even bigger than the one at Chesapeake Bay. For example, Chicxulub on the Yucatan Peninsula of Mexico has a crater which has a diameter of more than one hundred miles. In this case the asteroid could have easily been ten miles across. One can only imagine how high the waves would have been that propagated out from that location.

The height that a moving object can reach as well as the distance that it can travel is related to its speed. This relationship simply equates the kinetic energy of the moving material to the potential energy it would have at maximum height. For example, if any object was moving forward at five hundred mph it could reach a height of about eight thousand feet without any additional energy being required. This explains why the tsunamis that have a forward speed of 400 mph, pose such a serious threat. Never go down to the beach to watch a tsunami come ashore. This has been done with fatal consequences. If the moving water had a significant starting height, this would have aggravated the situation even further.

An example of the distance that a water wave can travel is provided by the explosion of Krakatoa in 1883. A Dutch sailor in the area reportedly heard the explosion and turned around to see a monster wave approaching. The ship was immediately swung around and it rode up the front of the wave 'at a steep angle'. An estimate was made of the wave height and taken to be about one hundred and twenty feet. This was a monster by any comparison. While the sound wave from that explosion measurably circled the world three times, the wave went as far as the English Channel.

Occasionally, the impact of an asteroid is simulated and shown on television. On these simulations it can readily be seen how high a wave can reach in comparison to the impacting asteroid diameter. Therefore, suggesting that a wave several miles high might propagate outward from a crashing asteroid is quite appropriate. An even more readily-available demonstration is available every day of the week at any Tim Horton's restaurant. Here a drop of liquid is seen dropping into a cup of similar material. Immediately a ring-shaped wave forms and propagates outward. Other waves also form but the primary wave is quite high in comparison to the size of the drop and it can therefore be more readily appreciated how high the waves could be from an object several miles in diameter and moving ten times the speed of a bullet. These demonstrations support the contention that a wave as high as Mount Everest could readily develop from a large asteroid hitting the ocean. How far would such a wave be able to travel, if a wave a little more than one hundred feet high could make it one-half of the way around the world? By this comparison, a wave several miles high would be expected to circle the Earth repeatedly.

During the Great Genesis Flood there would have been numerous examples of sheet flow movement, some of which would have been caused by the mountainous tsunami waves and some would have been produced by elevation of the ocean floor at the antipodes of impacting asteroids on the far side of the Earth. Others would have been generated indirectly by the massive earthquakes resulting from the impacts of asteroids with the crust of the Earth. Sheet flow and waves would have encountered sheet flow and waves. With all of the mayhem produced by all of the water commotion, being on the water at all would have been most hazardous. How then did the Ark survive? It certainly would not have been able to withstand very much bending. With the tumult of the intercepting water flows there would have been very few places on the Earth that any boat would have been safe. Therefore the question must be asked; was the Ark divinely protected? If that was indeed the case, it would have been an Element of Providence.

2.1.5 Water Burden during the Flood

Continent-crossing waves of water would have been impossible to deal with on their own but there was more than just water involved. Entrained in the water was an unending quantity of other material. Some of it would have been vegetable matter including entire forests of trees and other plants. This material would have been swept and rolled along and when the force of the flow was not quite enough to keep things moving these monstrous masses of vegetation would have stalled in great piles. Most of this material was subsequently buried and has now become coal. Coal is simply trees and other plant matter from which the volatiles have been removed leaving only the carbon. Numerous different types of trees have been identified in coal and they include trees that would normally be found on dry land well away from the ocean as well as trees that might have been part of a swamp. Different types of trees result in different types of coal.

As well as trees, the raging, crashing tumult of water also carried mountain-making material. Most of the mountains all around the world are formed from sedimentary rock. This is a type of rock that has been formed from material which has been placed by water. In some places these formations are thousands of feet thick. All of the material that forms these immense structures has been carried and deposited by moving water. And some of the material that was transported into place by the moving water has formed layers that are remote from mountains and have not formed sedimentary rock, as such, but rather simply appear as compressed material instead. Formations such as this can be seen at the Grand Canyon. Here, numerous layers are visible and it is understood that the material that forms these layers was placed by water.

The mountain-making material is of interest for two other reasons. Firstly, the thickness of the layers, which are often thousands of feet thick, tells us that the catastrophe that placed the material involved the entire world. It is simply not credible that the great commotion required to place several thousand feet of material on one continent had nothing to do with other continents. It would have been impossible to have that much activity restricted to just one area. This means that the material for all of the mountain ranges of the world was placed during one cataclysmic event. Secondly, we note that the layers of sedimentary rock in the mountains are often distorted from horizontal and bent both upwards and downwards. These formations are called synclines and anticlines. But how was this rock bent without braking? It is not possible to bend a rock formation that is five thousand feet thick without breaking it. The mountains are made of rock and rock does not bend very well. Appealing to long time spans does not help either because the amount of extension and compression required is several hundred feet. Rock cannot be bent that much. The logical explanation is that the rock was bent before it had a chance to harden. It was bent while it was still in a 'soft wax-like state'. This in turn means that it had to have been bent within a short period of time after placement which time could not even have been one year. After that it would have been too hard and brittle to bend without breaking. This agrees with Holy Scripture because it is stated in the Genesis account that the entire event only required one year. Was all of this correlating evidence from nature provided for our benefit? Was this an element of Providence?

A crashing roaring chaotic wall of fast-moving water would have been more than enough to contend with but when it also entrained vast amounts of soon-to-be-solid material it can readily be seen that survival of almost any type of boat would have not been possible. How did the Ark manage to avoid coming into collision with some of this solid, water-entrained material? The Ark was only made of wood. What would have happened if some small portion of the material that would soon form the layers of the Grand Canyon came into contact with the relative fragility of the Ark? Dealing with the crashing mountains of water would have been more than enough of a challenge for the Ark but also dealing with structures which included thousands of tones of semi-solid material would not have been possible. Was the Ark somehow shielded from these effects? Was the Ark kept in an area where this sort of trouble did not occur? Was the Ark divinely protected? Was this an Element of providence?

2.2 Temperature and Light

The temperature and light aspects of the Great Genesis Flood are closely connected even as these phenomena are closely connected at the present time.

Among the many devastating results of an impact, a great Earth-encircling cloud of dust and tiny rock fragments would be generated and rise from the impact location much like the mushroom cloud that is produced when an atomic bomb is exploded. This cloud would rise and spread out and keep right on spreading out until thousands of square miles were cast into darkness. Within a few days the entire Earth would become enveloped in this cloud which would not go away quickly. Various commentators state that it would remain intact for months and possibly even years.

The darkness resulting from this cloud would have been devastating. Morning would come but there would not be any sunrise. Night would come and there would not be any moonlight. It would be dark to such an extent that plants could not grow and nothing could be seen. It would be comparable to being down deep in a coal mine when the lights are turned off.

Some of the animals on the Ark would not have been upset by the darkness initially. How would they have responded after a month? Would they have been able to cope with darkness that continued for months?

Bees live in the dark. Inside a beehive there is very little light. The bees go about their activities as usual and do not appear to be concerned. However they expect morning to come. If it remains dark too long they become agitated. How would other creatures on the Ark have dealt with this? Could all of the creatures on the Ark have been able to placidly accept that it was continuously dark? Was some type of hibernation involved? When an animal is hibernating it really has no concern about whether it is dark or light. Many types of animals do hibernate. However, there are many that do not hibernate. Were all of the animals on the ark hibernating? Or had they been placed into some sort of state where they were motionless and stationary and not the least bit concerned whether it was dark or light? If so, would this have been an Element of Providence?

Temperature was also involved during the sojourn on the Ark and the temperature was not particularly favourable. It turned cold. Perhaps not the bitter extreme cold of the high arctic but much colder than any of the Ark's inhabitants had experienced before. After all, prior to being on the Ark all of the animals were accustomed to an environment that had temperatures well up in the comfort range. The entire Earth was warm prior to the Great Flood event so all of the animals would have been quite comfortable in a greenhouse setting but not in a walk-in freezer.

Of necessity, the animals would have been in close proximity to each other and this would have increased their comfort level when it was cold outside. It is not very likely that the Ark had any heating appliances. Even if there was, burning wood under such tumultuous circumstances would not have been wise. The easiest conclusion was that the Ark was unheated and that the animals were able to deal with the cold some other way. Going from plus 25C or 30C to minus even a few degrees would have necessitated some compensating factor to enable them to deal with that much temperature shift.

At this remote time, the darkness and cold can only be recognized and any actual compensating factors that could have been at work can only be hypothesized. Would any such factors have been Divine intervention? Were any of them Elements of Providence?

2.3 Contaminated Air

Every animal requires clean, uncontaminated air to breathe. Particulate matter and gaseous components in the air are particularly objectionable. Smoke is not acceptable.

During the Great Genesis Flood Event the entire Earth was in extreme turmoil. Asteroids were impacting the Earth every few hours. Immeasurable quantities of dust became elevated and permeated the entire atmosphere. Volcanoes erupted. Their effluent included not only dust but obnoxious gases as well.

A common component of a volcanic eruption is methane. There is an abundance of natural gas (i.e. natural gas is mostly methane) in the ground and when the ground is opened by almost any means, natural gas escapes into the air. In fact, this is happening continuously at the present time and will keep on happening into the future. Besides being objectionable, methane is a greenhouse gas and as a greenhouse gas it is many times as effective as carbon dioxide(CO_2) in retaining the Sun's heat near the surface of the Earth. The great Russian bogs started to melt in 2005 and have been melting at a great rate ever since. Thousands of tons of natural gas and

Methane have been released into the air. Thankfully it is still only a very small fraction of the total greenhouse inventory. However no matter how small a fraction of the atmosphere it represents, methane is simply not breathable.

How would any animal breathe air that was contaminated with objectionable gases as well as particulate matter? Even plants would not have been able to deal with this type of air and their micro-openings would have become clogged. The lungs of air-breathing creatures would not have had it any better. In the case of creatures on the Ark, they required clean air to breathe for an entire year. Were they fortunate in having the Ark in a preferred location? Was there some part of the Earth where the air was basically alright to breathe without worrying about being poisoned? Or was there divine intervention to provide breathable air? Was this intervention continuous throughout the animal's entire sojourn on the Ark? Would this have been an Element of Providence?

2.4 Preservation of Hull Integrity

As discussed above, the hull of the Ark had to be able to withstand bending and twisting for several months. Otherwise the occupants would have been spilled into the tumult. It also had to remain impenetrable to water seepage. This would have been a necessary feature of the hull's design and construction.

The hull was made of wood. The Bible says that it was pitched within and without with pitch. During the present age, we would probably refer to this material as tar. The tar would have been applied over all of the places where the planks and joints of the ark occurred. In fact it was applied over the entire surface both inside and out. This seems like a good idea and hopefully water would not get past the tar and seep through the cracks. However the Ark was a very large vessel. There were a great many places where joints in the wood could possibly have allowed water to enter.

Throughout most of the journey the hull of the Ark was subject to stress. It would have been twisted and bent and lifted up on every wave before slipping down the other side. Every joint where there was even a little bit of differential movement would have been a possible entry point for water. If the Ark had been shorter it would have been able to withstand these stresses much better but it was really a very long vessel.

Perhaps a little water did get in. If the food and water supply for the animals was running low, the Ark would have floated a little higher in the water and a little buoyancy-compensating water-seepage ballast would have kept it near the original level. If this had been the case, the Ark would have had a time limit on its usefulness. It could not have survived even a little bit of continuous seepage for an indefinite period of time. It would have sunk. Was the integrity of the hull of the Ark sustained by Divine intervention? Was this an Element of Providence?

3. Temperature Stability

The Earth enjoys a very high degree of temperature stability and temperature stability is not optional. It is absolutely necessary. The current average surface temperature of the Earth is very close to +15C. Certain measurements indicate that it is rising. Various estimates have been made concerning how much it might rise over the next number of years and the concern is often expressed that an increase of even a few degrees will cause widespread changes that will not be in our favour. A few degrees in this case is in the single digits and scientists express concern that a two-degree rise will be noticeable with changes in weather patterns, ocean circulation and the intensity of storms. Even at the present time when any temperature changes must be recognized as miniscule it seems that weather patterns are already changing. Flooding is reported where it is considered unusual and heavy snowfalls have also been reported in unusual places. The permafrost is melting in the far north and this is mostly perceived as a negative development. It has been the permafrost that has kept the land along northern coastlines in place since that land material was originally put in place. As the permafrost melts, the land is washed away and coastlines are being eroded. This is a very negative development where settlements are involved. Some changes due to changing climate admittedly appear benign such as the appearance of birds and animals further north than they would have been expected only a few years ago. However, some changes are viewed as being seriously negative.

The average surface temperature of the Earth has been measured now for many decades and this makes it clear that any change that is taking place is really quite small. Never-the-less quite small is quite alarming and a great deal of discussion has resulted with opinions understandably spread over a wide spectrum. Ongoing measurements and other observations will confirm or deny any changes. The basic underlying reality remains that if a change is taking place of even a few degrees, more change will be expected and the results of any significant change will be a major world-wide disaster.

All of this will result from a change in the surface temperature of only a few degrees. In recognition of this how could the Earth have possibly maintained a steady virtually-unchanging narrowly-regulated temperature for such a long time? Why would anyone expect that this could have been done for even a year or two? Any such expectation would really be quite presumptuous. Actually such expectations are benign – nobody really thinks about them at all. In fact, very few people would be thinking about it yet if it were not for the alarm bells being sounded by knowledgeable scientists all around the world.

3.1 Temperature Regulation Factors

The temperature of the Earth must be regulated. It must be actively controlled just like the temperature inside of a house during the winter. Several factors conspire to reduce the interior temperature of a house including cold outside air that seeps in around the doors and windows. When this happens, the furnace must be turned on or else the temperature will soon drop below the comfort zone. Turning on the furnace in response to a drop in temperature, is called regulating the temperature. It could also be called actively controlling the temperature. Just as the temperature of a house must be regulated, or controlled, to a very particular level for the comfort of the inhabitants, so too must the temperature at the surface of the Earth be held(or controlled) to a very particular level. A deviation of temperature in a house will cause discomfort for the occupants but a deviation of the temperature of the world would be disaster for all types of life on the Earth.

3.1.1 Heat from the Sun

It is pretty obvious that we do need heat from the Sun and we need an abundance of it. On a solar-system scale, Mars is only a little farther out from the Sun than the Earth but it is much too cold for life to exist. If any form of life, in particular human beings, was to arrive on Mars they would require a significant source of heat right from the outset. If the heat supply failed they would perish within minutes. While there have been several proposals for people to go to Mars, they would be dependent on a supply of heat for the entire trip. This would be a tall order and difficult to achieve. On the same scale, Venus is only a little closer to the Sun. No one will ever think of going to Venus. In fact it is difficult to even send down a probe. It is much too hot. In particular, the surface is so hot that it is not far below incandescence. Of course there are numerous other factors that rule out any visits to Venus but temperature is certainly one of them. It is clear then that the temperature that we require on the Earth is quite particular and it must remain very steady as well.

The basic starting point to achieve such a particular criteria is a rock-steady output from the Sun. In this regard the Earth is fortunate. The output of our particular Sun is very steady. Unfortunately the same cannot be said for many other stars which go into flare-up mode from time to time and would not be the least bit suitable as a heat source for a life-supporting planet.

While the output from the Sun must be perfectly steady, the distance between the Earth and the Sun is also very particular and must not be allowed to vary. To achieve this requirement, the orbit of the Earth around the Sun must be very close to circular. Any deviation from circular must be in our favour and this turns out to be the case. As our Earth orbits the Sun it follows an elliptical pathway that carries it out a little farther during part of the orbit and in a little bit during the other part. These deviations work perfectly in our favour because when the Earth is closer to the Sun our angle of inclination causes the heavily watered side (i.e the southern hemisphere) to be facing the Sun more directly. Therefore the incoming heat is absorbed and retained better. At the same time it would be winter in the northern hemisphere and we can always us a little more heat in the winter. Then, when the Earth is a little farther away from the Sun, the primarily-earth northern hemisphere is farther away from the Sun. This will be summer in the northern hemisphere and it means that our summers will not be quite as hot as they would be if the situation was reversed and the Earth was closer to the Sun at that time. We really do enjoy an excellent arrangement and anything different would be less favourable for us. The net result is that the minor changes in the distance to the Sun that occur over the course of a year are optimally accommodated by the material forming the Earth's surface. This is a most fortuitous situation to say the least but it does require a very predictable and absolutely-repeatable orbit.

However in spite of all of the stability factors that we enjoy, the Earth appears to be over-heating. It therefore seemed appropriate for some scientists to suggest that we try to intercept some of the heat that the Earth receives so it will not even reach the Earth's surface. There have been at least two suggestions to achieve this. The first one involved intercepting some of the Sun's heat far out in space. Large umbrella-shaped objects would be placed in space between the Earth and the Sun and they would prevent some of the heat from getting through. This would admittedly be a difficult achievement but was seriously being considered and probably will be considered even further if an overheating problem continues to develop significantly. A second proposal was generally in the same direction but instead of intercepting some of the heat far from the Earth it would be intercepted high in the atmosphere instead. Inserting material into the atmosphere would be much more readily achieved than trying to place it far out in space. This seemed logical until it was realized that this would change the thermal characteristic of the atmosphere and such a change would not be favourable. The downpours so necessary to tropical areas would not develop with drought and starvation happening instead. When a desperate situation appears to be developing, unusual ideas are bound to come forth and we cannot blame anybody for trying to find an answer. During the coming years we should expect other suggestions to come up to try to reduce the amount of solar heat that the Earth receives. In desperation some of them might be tried.

3.1.2 The Greenhouse Gases

Greenhouse gases are those parts of the atmosphere that are involved in regulating the surface temperature of the Earth. They are actually a critical component of temperature control and without them life on the Earth would not be possible. The Earth is only habitable if the surface temperature remains in between the freezing point of water and the body temperature of animals. In fact in consideration of the extreme temperatures that occur on the Earth near the poles and near the equator, the average surface temperature must remain very close to where it is at about +15C. This is approximately one-half way between the extremes. It is the current opinion of numerous scientists that if the average temperature drifted up to +20C or +25C life on Earth would be dramatically curtailed. It would be a world-wide disaster.

There are several gases in the atmosphere that are referred to as greenhouse gases. These gases all have the characteristic of capturing heat radiated from the surface and reradiating it back to the surface. Of course all heat comes to us from the Sun. When the Sun's radiation shines on the Earth's surface, some of it undergoes a frequency change. The frequency becomes lower and what arrived as visible light energy becomes heat energy which the atmosphere can absorb. So it is absorbed and sent back to Earth again. This is a critical factor in keeping the surface temperature right where it is and right where we need it to be kept.

The two most influential greenhouse gases are carbon dioxide (CO_2) and water vapour. There are several others as well but together they only account for a small percentage of the total effect. One of these is methane. Methane is understood to be about 25 times more effective than CO_2 as a greenhouse gas and unfortunately a great deal of methane is being released into the atmosphere every year. Much of it comes from the great Russian bogs which evidently started to melt in 2005. .The general warming of the Earth is credited for melting the permafrost in that area.

CO_2 is thought to be the cause of the current general warming trend. The level of CO_2 in the atmosphere started to measurably increase during the great industrial revolution. In order to generate steam for industrial production, coal was burned. In fact a lot of coal was burned and more and more of it has been burned every year since. Now we also burn oil and natural gas. As a result of all of this burning the level of CO_2 in the air has gone up. As it rises there is expected to be an increase in the average surface temperature of the Earth. While the actual change is really quite small, it is very influential. One of the results of an increase in CO_2 – if such an increase is causing the temperature to rise – is to make the air warmer. Warmer air can hold more water vapour and water vapour is an even more influential greenhouse gas than CO_2. Unfortunately the amount of water vapour in the air is solely dependent on the temperature of the air. This could become a viscous cycle where an increase will cause a further increase.

Another result which is self-aggravating is the melting of sea ice. When the water warms and sea ice melts, more ocean surface is exposed to direct sunlight. The albedo of open water is much lower than the albedo of sea ice so the Sun's energy is absorbed better. This means that the water will warm up even more and melt more ice. This cycle is much more time-limited than the self-generating cycle is for water vapour increase because there is only a relatively-small amount of sea ice to melt. When it's gone this particular viscous cycle will terminate.

The proper operation of the greenhouse gas temperature regulation system is absolutely essential to life on the Earth and without this control factor being actively at work our temperature would drift - to our initial discomfort and eventually to our annihilation.

3.2 Results of Temperature Change

If the average surface temperature of the Earth increases, ocean levels will rise. This appears to be happening already and is understood to be the result of both glacial melting and water expansion (i.e. due to being warmer). The rising water levels mean that livable land areas will be reduced. It also means that there will be a reduction in the world-wide food supply for items that would normally have been produced on the lost land. When the remaining glaciers are gone – in particular those in the Himalayas –the rivers that flow from these mountains and provide moisture for the food-producing deltas, will dry up. A great many people live on those river deltas, especially in Bangladesh and when the rivers through that area dry up, so will the capability of the area to produce food. Such major developments are suggestive that there will be attempts by large numbers of desperate people to relocate but this will likely be met by opposing forces most of which will be armed and resist any such migrations. In desperation wars could develop. All of these woes might have happened as ice age maximum was reached except that there were far fewer people on the Earth at that time and those that were would not have had time to settle the vast areas of ocean floor that lay exposed. The relocation of millions of people was therefore not necessary. The composition of the greenhouse gas inventory cannot be changed without terrible calamities developing.

Ironically, another effect of increasing temperature provides confirmation that the Earth has been through major upheaval followed quickly by the Ice Age. Along the northern coast of Russia the permafrost is melting. Every summer more of it melts with several very noticeable consequences. One of these is that as the soil can no longer withstand the action of the waves along the shore. As a result the shores are being quickly eroded away. Actually both the melting permafrost and longer seasons with open water (due to shorter seasons with the sea frozen) means that the waves have more time every year to erode the softer shorelines. In many places the shorelines are receding very noticeably and in some places islands are disappearing altogether. In such cases long-standing communities will have to relocate. In particular, this is the case with an island north of Alaska and it appears that the residential community on the island will have to leave for the mainland within a few years.

The other very noticeable result of the warming trend and one of even more interest for the present discussion is the exposure of tusks of the great Woolly Mammoth. These must have been magnificent creatures as their tusks alone are huge and curl out and around in a most majestic manner. The tusks are made of ivory which is a very useful material and for centuries it has been carved into a variety of useful shapes. Piano keys were once made of ivory. However to be carvable and hence useful, ivory must be fresh. Fresh ivory is ivory that was very recently part of a creature that was alive. It must either have been recently harvested from a recently-living creature or it must be quickly frozen as soon as the creature dies and kept frozen. If it becomes frozen almost immediately then it can be thawed out at a later time and carved just it can be if it is recovered from a recently-living animal. There is a market for fresh ivory but, unfortunately, to meet this market animals are killed illegally. This is a tragedy but the benefit is that there is a demand for the material and this motivates a small number of hardy men to venture to the far northern shores of Russia to prospect for the material along the places where the long-frozen permafrost is now giving up its secrets. Since only fresh ivory will do, the ivory that these people recover is readily marketable and apparently a reasonable living can be made by recovering even a few good specimens in a single season. It must be noted that the mammoth tusks recovered are not only fresh, they are very seldom ever found attached to an animal. They have been broken off. This indicates that these animals were caught in an event which killed them and carried them away in such a violent manner that their tusks were broken off. As they were carried away, so was the material that would very soon bury them. This would also indicate that a major upheaval was in process even if only a few tusks had been found but reports indicate that further along these same coastlines there are so many mammoth bones and tusks that the islands north of Russia in the Arctic Ocean are composed of only two things; bones and sand. How overpowering could any event have been that could carry away and bury untold thousands of tusks and bones of a huge and powerful animal? Then, immediately following burial, the entire assembly of tusks and burial material was frozen. The cold must have come suddenly. Further, it must have stayed cold right up until the present time or the ivory in those tusks would not still be fresh. To still be fresh it must have remained frozen throughout all of the intervening years. Now the Earth is warming up and the evidence of a major animal-killing and burying event (the assemblages of animal remains in other locations across these areas include the remains of many other types of creatures besides the great Woolly Mammoth such as rhinoceros, hippopotamus and elephant) has become available. All of this indicates that the Earth was supportive of a huge number of magnificent creatures which were suddenly killed, swept away, buried and frozen so quickly that any ivory in the mix stayed fresh. If a shower of asteroids had hit the Earth this is the exact scenario that we would expect. By the way, while it has been noted that the ivory is fresh, is there any way that this evidence has been provided specifically so that later investigators would have clear evidence of the Great Genesis Flood and the immediately-following Ice Age? Was this an element of Providence?

As the warming trend continues more permafrost will melt and more structural changes in topography will result. Will other evidences of the Great Genesis Flood become evident? How much more evidence is needed before we realize that since the Holy Scriptures are in complete agreement with the world of nature, we should accept without question that a world-wide flood occurred just as the Bible declares.

3.3 Temperature Regulation Disruption

Both the orbit of the Earth and the greenhouse gases would have been affected by an event as momentous as asteroids impacting the Earth. This would be true whether they came at widely separated intervals or in a shower. The impact of any significantly-sized asteroid would be a major world-wide disaster affecting numerous factors which enable life to exist and thrive on the Earth's surface. The impact of a shower of asteroids would be that much more of a world-wide calamity.

The widespread volcanic activity resulting from an impact would, at the same time that it would be causing a decrease in temperature, due to the dust cloud, be causing an increase in temperature due to all of the hot volcanic material being released.. All of the molten material that oozed and poured and exploded from the volcanoes would cause an increase in temperature. On the land most of the heat would radiate away into space but under water the hot volcanic material would cause the temperature of the ocean to increase. Since volcanic activity, (including igneous provinces, (openings in the Earth's crust where molten material has oozed up and spread around) underwater rifts, (long splits of cracks in the crust of the Earth where material from the interior has come out and piled up along both sides), and cone volcanoes)always involves hot molten material from the interior of the Earth , it can readily be seen that since this activity was world-wide there would have been a significant increase in the temperature of the ocean all over the world.

A shower of impacting asteroids would both directly, at the impact site, and indirectly at all of the volcanoes that would erupt, produce a world-enveloping cloud. This cloud would cause a serious drop in temperature around the entire world and would therefore be a matter of great concern. Even one large impacting asteroid would produce a cloud that would envelop the entire Earth. Such a cloud would cut off the heat from the Sun. The surface temperature over any land away from volcanic activity would drop. It is expected that it would drop to below freezing within a matter of hours. Plants would die and the lakes would freeze. There would not be any food to eat and there would not be any water to drink.

Either an increase or a decrease in temperature would affect the greenhouse gas inventory in the atmosphere and in either case upsetting the amount of greenhouse gas in the atmosphere would only further exaggerate the initiating change in temperature and just make things worse. The best plan is to not disturb this factor at all and simply leave it alone.

The only way to escape the serious consequences that would follow a disruption in temperature would be for the cooling factor and the heating factor to closely offset each other on a world-wide basis. Since the temperature that we require has such a narrow range of allowable variance one wonders how the necessary and appropriate balance could have been struck right through the entire flood event. Would this have been another Element of Providence?

4. The Ice Age

The Ice Age was a period of time when ice accumulated in massive glaciers across many square miles of North America, Europe and Asia. Antarctica, Greenland, Iceland and several other islands in the far north were also involved. On Antarctica the ice accumulated until it was two miles deep. There was a similar development on Greenland as well. Ice volumes are always compared to the amount of water from the ocean that would have been required for their formation. The total volume of ice in the Greenland and Antarctica glaciers, (which actually accounts for most of the volume of ice that still exists), would have required more than two hundred feet of ocean water. At glacial maximum another three or four hundred feet of ocean is thought to have been involved. These quantities are very large by any comparison which makes one suspicious that such developments must have been rare and involved some most unusual development. Hopefully such a development will not recur.

4.1 Popular Ice Age Theories

In order to have an ice age, cold would have been required because there obviously must be snow and snow necessitates that the temperature, at least over the land, be below freezing. On this point there has basically never been disagreement among those who comment on ice ages because it seems quite elementary that the temperature be below freezing for snow to form. Unfortunately, it has commonly been the case that cold alone was thought to have been sufficient. The sufficiency of cold to cause an ice age has been so widely assumed that it has dominated ice age discussions for numerous decades. In support of this belief, several ideas have been advanced to explain how the cold condition was caused. The most currently-dominant one was offered by a person named Milankovitch who assumed that whenever the Earth drifted a little farther from the Sun, (as certain of his mathematical models predicted) there would be an ice age. A variation of this idea would have the Earth passing through a 'cold' region of space. For example, if it drifted (along with the rest of the solar system) into a region where there was more space dust, the energy from the Sun would be reduced and the Earth would suffer a chill. Both of these ideas have some validity because if the Earth did drift out a little farther from the Sun, a chill would certainly result. Or if the Earth drifted through a region of space where there was an excessive amount of space dust, it would be reasonable to expect that the Earth would chill from this cause as well.

4.2 Actual Ice Age Requirements

The basic requirement to have an ice age is to get the water that will form the snow from the ocean to the land. The water must be lifted from the ocean, transported until it is over the land and then caused to fall on the land as snow. In order for water to be lifted out of the ocean it must evaporate. As it evaporates into the air, the air currents would carry it until it was over land where the vapour in the air would condense (if the air had been chilled to below freezing) and precipitate as snow. An enormous quantity of ocean water was involved in the formation of the great ice fields of the Ice Age and several commentators have weighed in on just how much would have been required. The estimates offered are usually in the range of three hundred to five hundred feet of ocean. This means that a layer of ocean water some three hundred to five hundred feet deep would have been removed from the ocean and relocated to the land. This would have been in addition to the more than two hundred feet of ocean water that is still tied up in the remaining glaciers. The total therefore that would have evaporated and would have left the ocean would have been in the range of five hundred to seven hundred feet. This was a very great amount of water and therefore it would have required a most unusual development to generate the required heat to cause such a thing to happen. It certainly would not have been a very common occurrence and can properly be recognized as an extraordinary happening. How could several hundred feet of ocean water have been removed from the ocean and placed on the land? To have such a thing happen once in the entire history of the planet would be unusual enough but to think that it could have happened repeatedly seems quite preposterous.

There are two conditions that must have happened for such an extraordinary event to occur. The ocean water must have been heated. In order to evaporate water, heat is always required. If there is no supply of heat even the water in a kettle on the stove will not evaporate. It will just stay in the kettle. In order to evaporate water at any time a large amount of heat is required. In fact it requires five hundred and forty calories of heat just to evaporate one gram of water. By comparison it only requires one calorie to raise the temperature of one gram of water by one degree. From another viewpoint it requires one hundred calories of heat to bring a gram of water all the way from freezing to boiling but it requires another five hundred and forty calories to boil it or evaporate it. Of course it isn't necessary to heat water all the way to the boiling point before it will evaporate but to cause it to evaporate at any temperature five hundred and forty calories per gram is always required.

The problem is compounded when we realize that all of the water that was evaporated would not have found its way directly to the ice fields. There wasn't any water traffic director indicating just where the moisture in the air would go. Some of it would have rained or snowed right back on the ocean and some of it would have rained on the land if some area of land wasn't quite cold enough to enable snow to form. Of course there isn't any way to determine how much of the evaporated water never made it to the great ice fields but to suggest that only a fraction would have actually formed snow is very realistic. If we allow that possibly only one-quarter of the total evaporant actually formed snow, then instead of the five to seven hundred feet that was required for the snowfields there would actually have been about four times this much water involved. This realistically means that it was quite possible that more than two thousand feet of ocean evaporated during the whole event. This would have been a stupendous amount but any explanation for the Ice Age must recognize this possibility. How could two thousand feet of ocean, or possibly even more than this, have been caused to evaporate? What was the source of the heat that caused such an enormous portion of the water in the ocean to evaporate? It can readily be seen that the release of enough heat to drop the level of the ocean several hundred feet, would be an exceedingly rare and overwhelming event.

4.3 Rarity of Ice Age Conditions

The conditions that caused the Ice Age to happen would not only have been rare they must have been sustained all the way through the critical period to enable ice age maximum to be reached or it simply would not have happened. This means that all of the water for the ice fields would have had to evaporate within a relatively short period of time. It also means that the prolific snow-production conditions had to be sustained for the same period or else the required volume of snow would not have fallen.

These conditions had to remain in place right through every summer otherwise the snow would not have been enabled to fall or to have been preserved when it did fall. After all, there cannot be an accumulation of snow if the snow that does fall simply melts. The vast majority of snow that falls must remain as snow or else there will not be any accumulation. The conditions that enabled and caused all of that evaporation must have been sustained through the time that was required for glacial maximum to be reached or else the hypothesized glacial maximum causing the ocean level to drop so far would never have happened and there would not have been any Ice Age.

The fallen snow could not have been allowed to melt. Since the temperature was probably just below freezing, if the Sun had been allowed to fall on it, it would have melted sooner or later at some time during the year. Therefore, it could not have been allowed to melt all through the year for all of the years that were needed to reach glacial maximum. This means that the energy from the Sun must have been blocked for that entire period which would have involved several decades at least. How was that achieved? On the one hand it will not work to allow the Sun to shine during the time that the ice was accumulating. On the other hand it will not work to block the Sun indefinitely or life on Earth will not be possible. Solar energy is needed at the proper time and in the proper amount or food cannot be grown and animal life cannot be sustained. While neither of these things would have been happening where the snow was accumulating for thousands of feet anyway, solar energy blockage was absolutely necessary for such areas.

4.4 Solar Energy Blockage

In order to have had a prolonged period of cold the energy from the Sun must have been blocked from reaching the surface of the Earth. If it had been allowed to shine at any time prior to ice age maximum, there couldn't have been accumulations of tens of thousands of feet of snow because the Sun would have melted it. (i.e. 5000 feet of ice requires about 60,000 feet of snow) Also, if there had been an interruption in cloud cover the great conveyor belt bringing the snow would have been interrupted because it was the clouds that brought the snow. An enormous accumulation of snow was required and it must have arrived while the ocean was still warm enough to evaporate at an unusually high rate. Blocking the Sun through the build-up period of the ice fields was crucial to having an ice age at all.

Two layers of cloud blocked the Sun and without both of these layers present the chill period would have been shorter. The massive dust cloud generated by the impacts and the volcanoes was the initial cause of the blockage. All dust clouds will break up sooner or later and the Sun will shine again. However in order to achieve the massive ice accumulations of the Great Ice Age, more time was needed than the dust cloud would probably have provided on its own. (Several commentators have suggested that the dust cloud would last for a year.) The moisture cloud that brought the snow would also have blocked the Sun and aided in the cooling effort. The two cloud layers worked synergistically and kept the Earth in virtually total darkness, at least over the regions where the snow was piling up in such vast piles. Probably both types of cloud would have dissipated over the lower latitudes relatively quickly but the accumulations of snow further north would not have been interrupted because the lower temperatures at the higher latitudes enabled snow to form for years after formation near the equator had petered out. Snow would continue to accumulate the in the northern regions because the conditions would have been ideal for such accumulation. The water was still relatively warm and there would have been enough cloud cover due to the exceptionally-high evaporation rates to keep the Sun from shining and terminating the ice accumulation process. By the time the ocean had chilled in the north and the evaporation rate had fallen off, the great glaciers of the Ice Age had reached their maximum and were several thousand feet thick. However, long before this happened the glaciers in the mid-latitudes had already started to melt.

4.5 The Cold Factors

The first factor required for an ice age is obviously cold. In order to have an ice age an abundance of snow is required. Snow will only form from the moisture in the air when the temperature is below freezing. This really seems pretty obvious but there is a restriction on how much cold is involved. If it is too cold, the air would not be able to hold very much moisture and so very little snow would be produced. In order to have the Ice Age however a great abundance of snow was required. In fact it requires about twelve inches of snow to form one inch of ice. Since the Ice Age glaciers were understood to be one or two miles thick it can readily be seen that a great amount of snow was needed.

Very little snow falls on the top of Mount Everest. At almost thirty thousand feet above sea level the air is quite thin at the top and so cold that only a small amount of moisture is available. If an abundance of snow is required the temperature must be much closer to 0C than it usually is on Everest. If an abundance of snow could form on Mount Everest and because it is very seldom above freezing, there wouldn't be any rock showing up there at all. It would all have been buried deep in snow many decades ago. On the other hand if snow had been forming at an abundant rate for hundreds of years it would have compacted into so much ice that the slopes leading up to the top would be very deeply buried in ice by now. While there are several slopes where ice forms, there isn't nearly enough of it to suggest that the mountain is a good ice producer. It is simply too cold.

The fact that very little snow can be produced at high elevations explains why the hypothesized movement of ice during the Great Ice Age is not explainable by ice thickness. The ice could not really get much thicker than the height of Mount Everest so it could not have moved outward because of its thickness. Ice that somehow was able to accumulate until it was five or six miles high would not be able to move out any further than the distance of its own height. Ice Age ice on the other hand was spread over thousands of square miles. It did not move into position. It simply formed in position.

In addition to being a poor producer of snow, very cold air would cause the ocean to freeze. If the ocean froze there would not be any production of snow at all. Further, if the Earth simply became chilled, the air would not be able to hold water vapour and the greenhouse effect of the water vapour would be lost. This would drive the surface temperature of the Earth even further down with the situation only stabilizing when any further reduction in temperature did not result in any further drop in the water vapour content of the air. By that time the surface layers of the Earth would be frozen solid with no hope of ever thawing them out. Unfortunately, most ice age theories do not grapple with this fact and so must be set aside as being incomplete or even invalid.

The Ice Age necessitated that the cold be widespread and persist right through Ice Age maximum. The dust cloud and the moisture cloud worked synergistically to achieve this condition.

4.6 The Heat Factors

The second factor required to have an ice age is heat. An enormous quantity of heat was required and it was produced from the volcanism stirred up because the asteroid shower fractured the crust of the Earth so extensively. The evidence shows that there was several types of volcanism but how much of it would have been stirred up by a single impact? It is doubtful if a single impact could have released the enormous amount of heat that was needed to heat the ocean enough to cause it to evaporate several thousand feet of itself. A single impact would have, without doubt, ruptured the crust of the Earth but would not have produced all of the igneous provinces and the material accompanying the underwater rifts as well as the cone volcanoes. An asteroid shower was required to produce all of these results and all of them would have been needed to cause the ocean to evaporate to the great degree that it did. However, a single hit would have produced a globe-encircling cloud that would have blocked the Sun. Thereby the chill factor would have appeared but there would not have been an offsetting heat factor. As a result, the Earth would have been driven into the deep freeze instead. A deep freeze is not an ice age but it would have been a life-terminating development because if the Earth was ever driven into the deep freeze the heat regulating effect of the water vapour in the air would be lost. The water molecules would be retained in the ice and not free to permeate through the atmosphere. Unfortunately there isn't any conceivable way that the Earth could recover from such a state.

It would have required a tremendous amount of heat to move several hundred feet of ocean water from the ocean to the great ice fields. Possibly five or six hundred feet of ocean found its way into the ice fields but this does not recognize the huge amounts of water vapour that never made it to the ice fields at all. In reality two thousand or three thousand feet of ocean would have evaporated in order for a fraction of this amount to have actually formed ice. It would have required an asteroid shower to release enough heat from the interior of the Earth to do this. Alternately it can be argued that since the Earth has experienced an ice age, there must have been an asteroid shower.

4.7 The Provision of Temperature Stability

It is completely ironic that the conditions that are required to have an ice age are exactly the same conditions that are required to ensure that the average surface temperature of the Earth will remain stable in the habitable range. As discussed above, the average surface temperature of the Earth must absolutely remain very close to a certain point or life on the Earth will not be possible. It is only convenient that we have invented temperature scales that meet our requirements. These scales have nothing to do with the maintenance of temperature. Of all of the temperature possibilities available, how is it that our temperature is exactly where it should be? Further, how did the average temperature stay exactly where it had to stay during the unimaginably-chaotic even tthat included the impacting of more than one hundred asteroids with the Earth? There would have been upheaval and chaos on all sides. Somehow through it all the average temperature of the Earth remained right where it needed to be to enable animal survival. Was this an Element of Providence?

Both heat factors and cold factors were required to produce the great Ice Age and both of these factors in exactly the right amount are also required for life to be viable. This could not have been an accident of nature or simply a very improbable circumstance occurring. However, if an explanation is needed we will be hard pressed to find one in nature. Could this have been an Element of Providence?

5. Orbital Change

There is a reasonable possibility that the orbit of the Earth has changed. Such a possibility is unthinkable to many scientists for good reason. The Earth is very large and as such it has a great deal of mass. It would be difficult to change the orbit of any planet as massive as the Earth. On the other hand, there is nothing to prevent the orbit from changing except the mass. The Earth is not restrained by anything other than its mass. The motion of all objects through the cosmos is influenced by the other objects either by the force of gravity or by actual contact. There have certainly been contacts. Many of the planets and moons of the solar system have obvious marks of impact and some of them like Mercury have such a massive impact mark that it makes one wonder why the orbit wouldn't have changed. Mars is included in this category because Mars has three very large impact marks indicating that large objects have crashed into it. Both Mercury and Mars have elliptical orbits further raising suspicion.

5.1 Impulse Transmission

An impulse is a burst of energy applied to a quantity of material. It is a bundle of energy that is transmitted from one moving object to another object - either moving already or simply stationary. When the wind blows across the surface of a lake, energy is transmitted into the lake water and waves are formed. This is not impulse transmission. An impulse involves a short well-defined amount of energy and it would be more like a stone being thrown into the water than to the wind blowing across the water over an extended period of time. When a pitcher throws a baseball towards a batter and the batter hits it, the ball will transfer an impulse of energy into the bat. If the bat is simply held out in a stationary position it will be knocked backwards and there will not be any chance of a homerun. However if the bat is also moving and it moves to meet the ball an impulse of energy will be transmitted into the ball. In a case like this it is a question of which object has the most energy. If the ball has more energy than the bat the bat will be knocked backwards. If they have the same amount of energy, the ball will be stopped and the bat will stop and nothing else will happen. However the intension of the whole exercise is to knock a homerun so the batter will move the bat as fast as he can toward the ball. Both the greater movement and the greater weight of the bat will result in a net impulse of energy being applied to the ball which might be great enough to send it out across the field for a homerun. Both the speed of the bat and the weight of the bat are involved. (The idea of sending the ball towards the batter as fast as possible has several implications including the idea that when the ball and bat connect, the ball will be distorted. This distortion is a means of storing energy with the net result that the ball can travel further. A similar energy-storage development occurs when an arrow is released from a bow. Energy is applied to the arrow so fast that it cannot instantly respond so it bends. This bending is a means of energy storage.) The bat is also said to have mass which is another way of saying that it consists of real material. Anything and everything that consists of material – either heavy or light – or even hardly noticeable, has mass. As long as an object is resting on the Earth it can be said to have weight but as soon as an object is away from the Earth or not really affected by the Earth it will be referred to as having mass. In all cases where we are interested in the movement of something, reference will always be made to its mass and not to its weight.

The Earth has mass. It has a lot of mass. The Moon also has mass but not as much as the Earth. All of the objects in space have mass and when calculations are done the mass of these objects will always be used. The Sun has a great deal of mass. There is a great amount of material in the Sun even though it is mostly just gas. If it were somehow possible to put the Sun on the scales its 'weight' would be millions of tons and many thousands of times greater than the Earth would be if it could be put on a scales.

Things that have a lot of mass are hard to move. The more mass that they have the harder it is to move them. Alternatively, if they are already moving, it will be hard to change that movement. For example it would be very hard to change the movement of the Earth. Apparently is has been changed however because the Earth has a wobble. This means that as it rotates on its axis the extended North Pole does not always point directly at any one location in the sky. It will instead describe a small circle in the sky. Of course we do not notice this wobble because it is much too small but is has been measured and described quite accurately. In fact there are several components to the wobble which is suggestive of the Earth having been impacted more than once. Just like a spinning top, which will wobble if it is struck, the Earth appears to have been repeatedly struck and the compound wobble resulted. If an impulse was transmitted to the Earth by a heavy rapidly-moving object like an asteroid, one of the results could be a wobble in the Earth's rotation.

In order to help clarify these concepts, let us imagine that we have come upon a very large rock that is about twenty feet (six m) high. Moving a rock this large would be very hard. We could try to throw a baseball at it but that would probably not move it. We could also try shooting at it with a rifle. Rifle bullets carry a lot of energy but it would not be very likely that the rock would move for that reason either. We could also try driving into it with a car. When cars are moving at high speed they can be said to have a lot of energy. In this case the car would suffer damage but the rock would not move very much. If it did move there might be a slight rocking after which it would settle back down as if nothing ever happened. However something did happen in all three cases. An impulse was transmitted from a moving object into a stationary object and if micro-measurements could have been made, we would find that there had been some movement – even in the case where the ball was thrown at the rock. In nature, energy is always preserved and preservation would be retained in all of these cases by the movement of the ball showing up in a very slight movement of the rock.

The entire situation would be dramatically changed if the huge rock was suspended by a cable from a high tower. If it was hanging from this cable and it was just clear of the ground there wouldn't be any friction with the ground. This means that any energy that was transmitted into it would not have to overcome the friction with the ground before movement would take place. With this in mind the above experiment can be carried out again.

For our second experiment let us obtain a very large reasonably-spherical boulder. We will choose one that is approximately eight meters (twenty-six ft.) in diameter. Eight meters can also be expressed as eight hundred centimeters. Now suppose that we wish to throw a rock at this large boulder and see what happens. Let us choose a rock that is about four centimeters in diameter. (These numbers are chosen for convenience.) This would be a rock that was a little less than two inches in size so it really would not look like much of a threat to the large boulder. Now we will plan to throw the small rock at the boulder but we want to do it in such a way that all of the energy of the little rock is transmitted to the big one. We simply do not want the small rock to just bounce off the big one but to convey all of its energy to it. In order to do this we will make a convenient opening in the big rock and direct the little one straight into this opening. Now we are ready to carry out our experiment but first we will load the small rock into a cannon, which will be able to direct the small rock towards the large one at a much higher speed. Even a good baseball pitcher can only accelerate a baseball to about one hundred mph whereas we are more interested in what will happen if the speed of our moving object was much higher. After all, we are trying to get a reasonable simulation of what would happen if a large asteroid impacted the Earth and large asteroids travel at very high speed. Even a slow one would be moving at ten times the speed of a bullet and of course some of them move much faster than this – even up to one hundred times the speed of a bullet. Because of their very high speed – which is high compared to anything on Earth – their energy content is very high. In fact it is unthinkably high. It is much higher than anything from our everyday experience.

Now we are ready to carry out our experiment and see if the small rock will be able to disturb the large boulder. Therefore we load the cannon and fire the small rock at the large boulder. The large boulder will move sideways, gain a little elevation and then swing back again. We could call this astounding. If the large boulder is unrestrained, the small rock will move it. We understand this result because of the energy of the small rock which would, because it was moving so fast, have had a very high amount of energy.

Now we can compare the diameter of the Earth with the diameter of the large boulder. The diameter of the Earth is approximately eight thousand miles. When we compare this to the diameter of the large boulder at eight hundred centimeters we can see that the small rock could represent an asteroid about forty miles in diameter. While this would be a very large asteroid there isn't really any way of telling how large some of the largest asteroids were because a large one will not leave a conventional crater on the surface of the Earth at all. It would simply punch right through the crust of the Earth and distribute its energy throughout the entire world. How can this be measured? Estimates of asteroid sizes can only be made when a crater is formed. Otherwise they are impossible to estimate. Formations such as the Takla Makin Basin in China, the Tenitz Basin in Kazakhstan and the Congo Basin in Africa make one wonder just how large some of the asteroids actually were. The Vredefort Crater in South Africa, the Sudbury Crater in Ontario the Manicouagan Crater in Quebec, the Chicxulub Crater in Mexico, the Czech Crater in Europe and the Chesapeake Bay Crater in the USA appear as though the impacting object went right through into the interior and opened a channel to the molten zone enabling the site to regain the general curvature of the Earth. If the asteroid did open a channel to the molten interior, the opening would likely become covered over with broken pieces of the Earth's crust and possibly parts of the asteroid. All of this material would bob and float until the molten portion near the surface cooled down and solidified. The Manicouagan crater is even higher in the center making it appear that some of the pieces that floated up were a little lighter than the average. Regaining the general curvature of the Earth would be exactly what one would expect if the entire region was flexible as it would have been if it was composed of numerous pieces of material floating on low viscosity material from underneath. How large the asteroid might have been in each case is totally unknowable. We must also note at this point that there are still a large number of asteroids orbiting the Sun that have diameters greater than one hundred miles and it has even been admitted that no one knows where all of them are. Some commentators have even suggested that several of the objects that hit Mars would have been in this very-large category. If this was the case with Mars, why couldn't something similar have been expected on Earth?

When the rock-boulder experiment is compared to an asteroid impacting the Earth it is readily seen that the asteroid will impart an impulse to the Earth and instead of just pushing it sideways it will add its energy of movement to the energy of movement of the Earth. When the masses of the two objects are added up the total resultant mass would be virtually the same as before. But when the energies are added up there will be a noticeable increase in the energy of the larger object. In the case of the Earth, it would speed up a little bit and this would push it into a slightly higher orbit. With a slightly higher orbit, it would take a little longer for the Earth to complete one orbit around the Sun. If several large asteroids hit the Earth, the length of the year could possibly have changed from three hundred and sixty days to the three hundred and sixty-five and one-quarter that we have now.

Asteroids usually orbit the Sun in the same direction as the Earth. This means that they would, in all likelihood, approach the Earth moving through space in the same direction as the Earth. This means that if the Earth was hit, it would speed up a little bit. We understand that the Earth is not really constrained in space. It isn't tied down to anything. It is basically just heavy and difficult to move. It is recognized that some asteroids move in the opposite direction to the Earth and so would come in from the front. However this situation is mostly restricted to very small asteroids which more easily suffer orbital changes due to the influence of other heavenly bodies. Of course comets can approach the Earth from any direction at any time and are therefore much less predictable.

Now we can extend our argument a little further when we recall that the Earth has been struck by more than one hundred asteroids. This many impact sites have already been confirmed and we can speculate that because the Earth is widely covered by either vegetation or water there are very likely more impact sites as yet undiscovered. Locations that look suspiciously like impact sites are actually visible at the present time but have not yet been 'officially' identified.

In this regard one wonders about the Congo Basin in Africa, the Tenitz Basin in Kazakhstan and the Takla Makin Basin in China. If these are actually asteroid impact sites the monsters that formed them would have transferred a very noticeable impulse to the Earth and its orbit would have been changed. But, as discussed above, it is clear that its orbit cannot be changed without dire consequences.

5.2 Asteroid Shower on the Earth

The mountains of the Earth testify to an asteroid shower having happened. All of the mountain ranges of the Earth are formed from sedimentary rock. The material for this type of rock would have been placed by water. While wind also produces sedimentary rock the formations that result from wind are usually quite small by comparison to the formations that water movement produces.

The direct physical cause of the Genesis Flood was the impacting of a shower of asteroids with the Earth. An expanded reasoning for this conclusion is discussed at length in the predecessor volume to this one; The Window of Life, A Theory of the Earth Based on Asteroid Impact. A brief review of that reasoning is included here.

Any asteroid impact of significant size would be a world-wide disaster involving the extensive rearrangement of the Earth's surface. Mountains would be formed and the material for the future coal beds would be transported and put in place. Land-based animal life would be wiped out because there would be no land to provide either shelter or sustenance. It would be completely dark for several months. The temperature would drop and the surface layers of the Earth would freeze solid. Two other factors at play would be the exposure of large areas of previously-unexposed rock as well as an increase in the ability of ocean water to absorb CO_2. After the ocean was heated by under-water volcanic activity, it would start cooling which would expectedly take several years. As water cools it absorbs more CO_2. With both the freshly-exposed rock and the cooler ocean, the CO_2 content in the air would diminish. Since CO_2 is a greenhouse gas, by removing it from the atmosphere, the temperature of the Earth would drop even further and this would enhance the freezing brought on by the heavy cloud cover. Under such circumstances, if any surviving animal had come across some food, it would have been frozen so hard that it would not have been possible to eat it anyway. Obnoxious gases would be released into the air making breathing very difficult or completely impossible. The continents would be repeatedly overrun by monster tsunamis coming from the oceans.

Asteroids were raining down on the Earth. Many of the large ones would have formed a crater as they smashed through the crust of the earth into the interior. Some of the material that was dislodged to form the crater would have left the area and rained down on the surrounding country-side for hundreds of miles. Many of these would be identified later as Erratic Boulders. Erratic Boulders (or Erratics) are rocks that appear completely out of place. Current popular thinking claims that they were moved into position by moving ice. However there has never been an explanation of how Ice Age Ice moved. On the other hand it is quite readily seen how an asteroid upon impact would produce a shower of boulders and other debris and cause it to be spread far and wide from the impact site. Erratics are found all over the world. In some places they almost completely cover the country-side. Erratics across the northern USA are understood to have come from Canada. A similar situation exists in Europe. The glaciers of the Great Ice Age did not do this but the impacting asteroids did.

While all of this was happening, the Ark was still afloat. How did it avoid being hit by one or more of the flying erratic boulders? Was it located in an area that was free of these flying objects? Was it somehow protected from being hit some other way? Was the Ark being divinely protected? Was this an element of Providence?

While it is virtually impossible to visualize how anything could survive such abuse, it is totally impossible to explain how the Earth could go through traumas of such magnitude and still expect any form of life to be found. Numerous commentators have been quick to suggest that only 5% or 10% would survive a single large impact but they have never offered any explanation whatsoever as to how this could have happened. If 5% did survive it certainly would not be 5% of every species. Animals never spread out evenly around the Earth but are more readily found in regions according to specific habitant and climate. This means that for any such survival scenario to be true, a great deal of evolution would have to take place between impacts. The surviving cohort from each impact would provide the starting point for the restoration of all animal life before the next impact. When that process was well underway another asteroid would arrive and everything would be set back again. Any scenario like this is not credible at all.

If, as is widely suspected, the asteroids formed by the explosion of a previously existing planet, most of them and certainly all of the large ones would be orbiting the Sun in the same direction as the Earth. The explosion which caused their creation would have spread them out. Some would have gone into higher orbit. Some would have gone into lower orbit and some of these might have spiraled in towards the Sun. With the explosion taking place between Mars and Jupiter, the swarm would have crossed Mar's orbit months before crossing Earth's orbit and this explains why the impacts on Mars are all on one side. The swarm did not yet have time to spread out and neither did Mars have time to rotate to spread out the impacts. By the time the swarm crossed Earth's orbit months or years later, it had spread out. Therefore as the swarm arrived in Earth's vicinity, Earth had time to rotate to spread the impacts all over the surface but the incoming direction would always have been the same.

5.3 Asteroid Shower on the Moon

The Moon has also been struck numerous times by very large objects. At least that is a reasonable conclusion from the evidence that is available. This evidence includes the observations that there are several flat craterless regions on the Moon and that all of them have, beneath their surfaces, mass concentrations. The third piece of evidence is the chaotic elevated terrain on the opposite side. Also, the far side is bulged away from the Earth and conventional attempts to explain this bulge appeal to tidal effect. Tidal effect is certainly a reasonable explanation once the bulge was generated but it would not explain the bulge in the first place even though attempts have been made to do this. However If the far side of the Moon somehow became bulged, the reduction of gravity from the Earth would help to keep the bulge in place. However an explanation for its formation in the first place is sorely needed and can be obtained from recognition that the Moon suffered numerous large impacts on the near side. Every one of these impacts would have generated an internal shockwave which would have travelled through the Moon and pushed up under the far side. Once it was elevated it would tend to just stay put. With a tide there are always two bulges; one on the side nearest the tide-inducing body and another one on the opposite side. On the opposite side the pull of gravity is reduced below average so the material of that side is even less attracted to the pulling body and so just slumps further away. Therefore if a bulge was caused to form on the far side of the Moon (e.g. because of shockwaves coming from the other side) there would be a reduced force trying to pull it back down so it would just tend to stay bulged. This would be especially true if the interior was molten or at least semi-molten. This must have been at least partially the case with the Moon because the Maria appear as the result of molten material coming up and spreading around.

Also, the major impacts must have happened within a short period of time because there are no impact sites of any consequence in the Maria. If some of the Maria were old, they would be expected to have more impact sites on their surfaces but they only have a few small ones at most. The lava simply spread around, cooled off and no more impacts of any significant size have happened in these areas since. This is not to say that there have not been other impacts. There certainly have been and one of significant size occurred in 1178 and was witnessed by a group of Monks who had decided to observe the Moon that night. They reported that 'fire shot out, the Moon turned black and shuttered'. Later the impact site was identified as being just over the visible edge. The blackening of the Moon was across the visible portion as there was only about one quarter of the Moon's surface showing that night. While there have been other impacts, this one is of particular interest because of its size and because a shower of meteors occurred on Earth a few months later. However, the event of primary interest for our present discussion is the asteroid shower that formed the Maria and caused the bulge on the far side.

The next question is whether or not that event would have changed the Moon's orbit. If the impacts all came from the same direction and if they happened over a period of a few days, the aggregate impulse would have probably changed the Moon's orbit. This is simply because they would all have approached the Moon during a small portion of its trip around the Earth and the Moon would consequently have been repeatedly nudged forward in its orbit. However if the shower of asteroids had been spread out over several months, the Moon would have had time to orbit the Earth several times. It would therefore have been approached from all directions with respect to the direction of its own movement. The net result in this case would probably be that its orbit wasn't measurably changed at all.

The movement of the Moon around the Earth is not of particular concern to most people but it is crucial to our survival that the Moon has a very stable and almost perfectly-circular orbit. In addition to being a convenient light on a dark night, the Moon provides two types of stability for the Earth. The first is orbital stability. The Moon is quite large when compared with the relative sizes of other moons in comparison to their planets. The comparatively-large size of the Moon means that the gravitational bond between the Earth and the Moon is very strong. Therefore as the Moon orbits the Earth the combination of Earth and Moon acts like a tightly-coupled system and the orbit of the Earth is thereby stabilized. It is very important that the Earth maintain a stable circular orbit. The strong gravitational link between the Earth and the Moon enhances this stability.

The second stability function that the Moon provides concerns the inclination of the Earth's axis. Since the Earth's axis has an inclination, the Earth has seasons. The pattern of the seasons matches perfectly with the slight eccentricity of the Earth's orbit to provide an ideal distribution of sunlight over the entire planet all year. However the Earth's angle of inclination must be held constant over long periods of time. If this were not the case it would drift back to zero and there wouldn't be any seasons. The dependable repeatability of the Moon's movement gives the Earth a dependable seasonal arrangement.

One is caused to wonder how the orbit of the Moon could, on an ongoing basis, be virtually ideal as a stabilizing factor for the Earth on its orbit around the Sun. Also why does the Moon orbit the Earth with a virtually-circular orbit in an orbital plane which causes the Earth's inclination angle to be exactly what the Earth needs to have the seasons that are so necessary for the Earth to habitable? After having been so severely pummeled by numerous asteroids, this seems totally improbable. Was this an element of Providence?

5.4 Other planets

5.4.1 Mercury

Mercury might not have suffered an asteroid shower but it certainly took a major hit. The Caloris Basin on Mercury is about eight hundred miles across. This is about one-quarter of the planet's diameter. If a comparable event occurred on the Earth, the diameter of the crater would be about two thousand miles. The Caloris impact would have generated a major shockwave which would have been expected to travel right through the planet to the other side and seriously disturb the surface. The side opposite Caloris is certainly disturbed and has an extensive area of chaotic terrain which is sometimes referred to as weird terrain. We also note that Mercury has a very elliptical orbit. This is understandable because the energy of the relatively-large fast-moving asteroid would have been added to the energy of the planet's motion and a modified orbit would result.

5.4.2 Mars

Mars is not hot and has very little atmosphere so, except when a sand storm is blowing, the surface can be observed quite well. On one side there are three very large impact sites varying from about five hundred miles in diameter to about one thousand miles in diameter. More or less directly opposite around on the other side there is a bulge which is elevated several kilometers above the average Martian surface. There are also numerous very large volcanoes one of which is thirty-seven kilometers high as well as broken chaotic terrain which includes a huge trench together with its expansion cracks (graben) running out from both sides. It appears that the shockwaves from the impacts traveled through the interior and violently disturbed the other side lifting and breaking the surface before slumping back into a widespread area of broken and chaotic terrain. In addition to the three major impact sites on the 'impact' side there are more than three thousand other craters that are more than twenty miles in diameter. This compares to less than three hundred on the chaotic side. It appears that all of the asteroids arrived within a relatively short time period and Mars did not have time to rotate enough to spread out the impacts more evenly around the entire planet. Mars has a very elliptical
orbit. Could this be the result of the many impacts that happened on Mars? Alternately, if the impacts had happened randomly over a great number of years, would the orbit be so elliptical now?

Mars has two moons but they are quite small and appear like asteroids. Certain commentators refer to these moons as asteroids which seems reasonable since they both appear to have been cast into space in a semi-fluid state just as one would expect if a planet with a partially-molten core exploded. The small size of these moons, the way that they orbit and the fact that Mars does not have either an equatorial bulge or a tidal bulge means that the angle of inclination of Mar's axis will drift. While life on Mars is impossible due to a total lack of environmental support factors, having an axis of inclination that is not stable only confirms that it could not have supported a life-enabling environment anyway.

5.5 Aggregate Impulse

An aggregate impulse (i.e. the impulses from all of the impacts added up because all of them would have approached the earth from behind) was applied to the Earth and this impulse changed its orbit slightly Coincidentally there is evidence in ancient literature suggesting that the Earth once had a three hundred and sixty day year. At he present time, the year is about 1.4% longer than this and it is tempting to explain the difference by a shower of impacting asteroids applying an aggregate (or additive) impulse to the Earth. If this was the case and the length of the year did change at the time of the Great Genesis Flood, a new problem presents itself. The incoming heat from the Sun would have changed. This means that the temperature regulation function provided by the greenhouse gases would also have changed. Hence one would expect a change in the climate of the Earth. The amount of any change cannot be calculated with any certainty nor can the amount of any change that might have occurred in the orbit of the Earth. (A much more detailed discussion of this factor is included in Fairytales for Adults, Theories of the Earth in Disarray'.) However the requirement for very strict control of the Earth's temperature causes one to pause. How could we have such a very-close-to-optimum orbit after suffering the aggregate impulse from a shower of asteroids? Was this an Element of Providence?

5.6 Goldilock's Orbit

The orbit of the Earth around the Sun has been called a Goldilock's orbit. It is 'just right'. The Earth does not get too close to the Sun and it does not get too far away. The variation that does occur is exactly in our favour. It has been speculated that even a 5% deviation in our orbit either way would be disaster. The orbit is always the same. There isn't any noticeable deviation from year to year and it almost seems like the Earth is moving through space on a steel track. Even the small deviation from circular that does exist is to our particular advantage. Any orbit so favourable to life cannot be an accident. It is just too improbable for it to be an accident. Was this an Element of Providence?

The axis of rotation of the Earth is not at ninety degrees to our plane of rotation around the Sun. It is tipped up several degrees. This tip-up provides the Earth with an 'angle of inclination' and four seasons of the year result. Having a year with seasons is a much better arrangement than having the Sunshine down directly on the equator all year but hardly on the polar regions at all. Without an angle of inclination all of the areas of the Earth with latitudes of more than about forty-five degrees would be below freezing most of the time and hence not very habitable. The angle of inclination of the Earth's plane of rotation enables a much greater area of the Earth to be habitable. If the Sun shone directly on the equator all the time the lower latitudes would be too hot for human habitation. In fact without an angle of inclination the habitable zone would be restricted to the areas between about the thirtieth parallel of latitude and about the forty fifth parallel of latitude on both sides of the equator.

Suppose that the angle of inclination was forty-five degrees instead of twenty-three and one-half degrees. With such an arrangement the Sun would drift north every year until it was over the forty-fifth parallel. On June 21 the Sun would therefore shine straight down across the northern USA and Southern Canada. This would give residents of these areas a very warm summer. The lakes would warm up, the crops would grow and we would have a different diversity of migratory birds. All of this would seem like a good idea but it wouldn't be a good idea at all. It would also mean that during the winter the Sun would be very low in the sky and basically right down on the horizon. This means that the Arctic Circle would be right across the northern USA. There would be very little heat from the Sun and winters would be extreme. The Polar Vortex would settle down over Southern Canada and stay there for many weeks. Spring would be late, The Lakes would remain covered with ice and the growing season would be brief. In short, Canada would not be very hospitable to life and it would be difficult to live there at all. During winter at the present time, the Sun does sink in the sky but it remains well above the horizon so winters are quite tolerable. Then when Spring comes the growing season is expected to be several months long.

Having no angle of inclination is very undesirable and having it at forty-five degrees is also far from desirable. It appears that our current angle of twenty-three and one-half degrees is close to optimum. Anything else would be less desirable. Was this provision an Element of Providence?

In order to retain this particular advantage, the angle of inclination must be stable and not change at all year after year. It must be as stable as the Earth's orbit around the Sun. This required stability is provided by the movement of the Moon around the Earth. It is the pull of the gravity of the Moon that maintains the angle of inclination and in fact it is the pull of the Moon's gravity that has produced the angle of inclination in the first place. The Moon has caused the angle of inclination and now it is maintaining it exactly where it is presently found and exactly where it provides maximum benefit to the Earth. Could this have just happened coincidentally?

As the Earth rotates and because it is mostly a giant ball of viscous fluid, it bulges at the equator. This bulge is simply due to the rotation speed and the fact that the Earth is not a solid ball of rock. The spinning action therefore causes a bulge to form at the equator and the size of this bulge is significant. At the equator the distance from the surface to the center of the Earth is about fourteen miles further than it is at the poles. There is also a second bulge involved. The tidal bulge is pulled up by the Sun and the Moon. These bulges provide something for both the Sun and the Moon to tug on. The gravitational forces equalize when the Earth's axis is twenty-three and one half degrees above its orbital plane and they therefore cancel out. The result is that the Earth keeps on rotating the same way with its present angle of inclination. The tidal force, the spinning Earth and the gravitational pull of both the Sun and the Moon result in a stable angle of inclination and a four-season year with the best possible arrangement for life on the Earth. Was this arrangement the result of chance or was it an element of Providence?

The arrangement has positive stability. That means that if the angle of inclination was somehow forced away from its optimal position, it would quickly be returned to that position. If it was reduced, the gravitational pull on the equatorial bulge would be reduced so the pull on the tidal bulge would increase and the angle would be restored. If the angle increased, the gravitational pull (actually torque) on the equatorial bulge would increase so the angle would be restored. In this manner there is no worry that anything will drift because if there was drifting either way restoration forces would take over and re-establish the correct angle. There is one further factor involved. There is a five degree difference between the Moon's orbital plane and the Earth's orbital plane. This small difference would have enabled the angle to have been established in the first place. If the pull of the Sun and the Moon had been exactly lined up, a case can be visualized where the angle of inclination might not have developed. There are too many factors involved with all of this for them to have just happened by chance. Any coincidental arrangement of so many factors is just not believable. Was there an element of Providence throughout the entire affair?

To retain this optimal arrangement, the Earth must orbit along the same track every year and the Moon must remain at the same distance from the Earth all the time. Is it coincidental that the Earth's spin, the Earth's orbit and the Moon's orbit all work together in exactly the right way to keep our favourable four-season arrangement? Could an arrangement like this have just happened by chance? Why was the Moon provided with exactly the correct mass and exactly the right orbit to exactly balance the pull on the bulges of the Earth when the angle of inclination reached twenty-three and one-half degrees? Was this arrangement an element of Providence? Was the Moon just drifting by on its way to who-knows-where one day and was just captured by the Earth coincidentally? How is it that the stability of a multi-part function that is so necessary for both our survival and the survival of all other forms of life on the Earth is just there and quietly operating year after year without having somehow been planned all along? How could such a particular and optimal set-up have happened at all? Will something like this ever be found on another planet? Was this arrangement provided for our particular benefit alone? Was this an Element of Providence?

The present orbit of the Earth acting together with the inclination of the Earth's axis evens out the temperature of the Earth in an optimal manner. The heat absorbing ocean faces the Sun when we are closer to the Sun. This is winter in the Northern Hemisphere and while the northern hemisphere is then tipped away from the Sun it is actually closer to it. We therefore receive a little more heat during our winter than we would have if we were further away at that time. During the winter we can always use a little more heat. Then during the summer while we are tipped toward the Sun in the north, we are actually further away from it and over-heating is therefore minimized. This is another most fortuitous situation. Why does the elliptical pathway of the Earth's orbit (that enables this to happen) remain the same year after year? How could such an optimal arrangement have resulted after the major upset of the arrival of more than one hundred asteroids? Was this also an Element of Providence?

The mass of the Earth is so great it would take a considerable force to change it and this is very much in our favour. In addition to the stabilizing factor of the Earth's size there are several other stabilizing factors involved. First there is the Moon. The Moon is coupled to the Earth by a very strong gravity bond. As the Moon orbits the Earth it acts like a heavy ball held by a rope and swung around by a person. The Earth-Moon system is a gravity-coupled system and hence more difficult to upset just as a person would be more difficult to upset if he/she was swinging a heavy ball around and around. It is also understood that Jupiter has a stabilizing influence on the Earth's orbit. While Jupiter is very large and any stabilizing factor that it provides would be significant, it has even been postulated that all of the planets have a stabilizing influence on the Earth's orbit. The total number of factors that might be involved in the Earth's stability can probably never be known but there appears to be several of them with the final result that the Earth has an exceedingly stable, optimal, Goldilock's orbit. Is this an Element of Providence?

Just when it appears that things could not get any more coincidental than they are, they will. It is also a fact of science that the Moon is drifting away from the Earth. As the Moon orbits the Earth it pulls up the tide. The tide shows up as a moving bulge which would be lined up directly with the Moon except that the Earth is spinning relatively rapidly on its axis. As a result of this spin the bulge does not reach maximum height until it is slightly ahead of a lime drawn through the center of both the Moon and the Earth. The tidal bulge therefore pulls the Moon ahead a little bit in its orbit causing it to climb a little higher all the time. By this means the Moon gets a little further from the Earth every year. By and by in the future, the Moon will be about one and one-half times as far away as it is now and its orbital speed will match the rotational speed of the Earth because the Earth's rotational speed will have reduced as the Moon receded. At that time the Moon will remain almost stationary above one particular location on the Earth and the tidal bulge due to the Moon will no longer travel around the Earth. Unfortunately a day on Earth at that time will be about two weeks long and a night will be about two weeks long and life on Earth will seriously curtailed. Also the Moon's greater distance will mean that it will not pull quite so hard on the Earth's bulges. The angle of inclination will consequently be reduced and the seasonal pattern will be modified. These two developments mean that life on Earth will become virtually impossible. How is it that we have the Moon at exactly the correct distance to enable seasons to happen at all? How is it that this 'window of life' that the Moon's distance provides ever even happened because if the Moon was closer, as it would have been in the past, another great set of calamities would result? Why is it that the Moon is at exactly the right distance for life on Earth to be sustainable even though that distance is changing continually? Is this an Element of Providence?

5.7   Provision of Temperature Stability

It seems that the orbit of the Earth was close to ideal before any trauma developed because it was habitable from pole to pole. Then the asteroids struck and they undoubtedly changed the Earth's orbit by some amount. It seems however that we once again have an ideal orbit so much so that it is referred to as a Goldilock's orbit. It is a just-exactly-right orbit. The amount of any orbital change as a result of asteroid impact can never be known but with the large number of known impact sites around the Earth and the certainty that all impact sites have not been identified yet makes it reasonably certain that the orbit was changed by some amount. If there had once been a three hundred and sixty day year, in order to get to a three hundred and sixty-five and one-quarter day year it would have been necessary to have an orbit change of about 1.36%. While this does not seem like very much in light of the orbital eccentricity of both Mars' and Mercury's orbits, it appears that we might have gotten through the whole affair better off than our heavenly neighbours. Getting through relatively unscathed was absolutely necessary because even a very small change in our orbit could have put us into a location that would not be at all favourable to life. The temperature of the Earth must be very tightly regulated at just the correct level or it will drift into a region where life activities will be either curtailed or terminated. While admittedly, any orbital change would have been small, how is it that our temperature has remained so very close to ideal? How could this have resulted after so much upheaval? Was this an Element of Providence?

6. The Greenhouse Gases

As mentioned above, greenhouse gases are those components of the atmosphere that have an influence on the surface temperature of the Earth. Also, as mentioned, they are not optional but are absolutely essential. Life on the Earth would not be viable without the temperature-stabilizing influence of these gases. All down through the years there did not seem to be much concern or interest in them but since it was realized that one of the most influential of these gases, carbon dioxide (CO_2), was increasing substantially, the alarm bells started going off. There is valid reason to be concerned. As a greenhouse gas, CO_2 absorbs some of the heat being radiated up from the Earth's surface and re-radiates it right back to Earth. As a result the temperature of the Earth remains very steady right through any particular twenty-four hour period and stays in the comfort zone. Without such a stabilizing factor there would be a much greater temperature variation between day and night as well as a much lower average temperature. This would not work very well in winter but the colder weather resulting would make it even worse during the summer. Crops must be grown. Vegetation must thrive. If there was frost almost every night all year, very few plants would survive.

Significant temperature variation between day and night can currently be experienced on the Earth even near the equator. On the Sahara Desert it is not uncommon to have frost at night. This can even happen when it has been at the upper limit of the comfort zone during the day. The explanation usually relates to the dryness of the desert air. The lower amounts of water vapour allow heat that is being radiated up from the sand to escape into space. Quite often so much heat will escape that the temperature will drop until it is below freezing. This means that temperature change between day and night can easily be more than 30C and such a variation would generate extensive mayhem in other parts of the world.

In general, as long as the greenhouse gases didn't change, they received very little attention. However CO_2 has been increasing steadily for the last few hundred years and has now reached levels not anticipated even a few years ago. It has not only gone up but the rate of increase has also gone up. It is increasing at an increasing rate. It seems to be running away and carrying the surface temperature up with it. Numerous scientists have therefore raised an alarm.

Just to make matters worse, there are several factors which have a self-sustaining, compounding effect. The first of these is the effect an increase in temperature has on the water vapour content of the air. Actually water vapour is the most influential greenhouse gas and is more influential than CO_2 over many parts of the Earth. Water vapour also traps heat and re-radiates it back to the surface but the problem is that the quantity of water vapour in the air is determined itself by temperature. This means that an increase in temperature caused by any other factor will result in an increase in water vapour. The temperature would therefore increase again due to the increase in water vapour and such an increase would result in even further increases in temperature. Once such a cycle gets started the temperature would continue to increase until the amount of water vapour could not increase any further. Until that point was reached, we would have a vicious cycle in operation. A similar type of situation arises if the temperature of the ocean increased. The ocean is very cold and the temperature of most of the water is very close to freezing. As such it can retain CO2. However if it warms up it cannot retain as much and the CO2 will start coming out. As with the compounding effect of an increase in water vapour, an increase in CO2 will result in more warming and more warming will result in more CO2 escaping from the ocean into the air. These factors could help to explain the change in the rate of increase of CO2 and some scientists suggest that due to developments such as these it wouldn't really matter if any more coal or oil was burned because now that the situation has been disturbed, the temperature will just keep on going up anyway. This is a most disturbing scenario to say the least.

There are other factors involved as the Earth warms and one of these is Methane. Methane is also a greenhouse gas and there is a lot of methane held in the crust of the Earth due to permafrost. As the permafrost melts this inventory of Methane will bubble out. In particular the great Russian bogs started to melt in 2005 and billions of tons of Methane have now been released. Fortunately to this point Methane is still a minor greenhouse gas.

As temperature stabilizers the greenhouse gases behave similarly to the ocean. The surface temperature of ocean water changes very slowly. Even if the Sun shines straight down all day the temperature of the surface layers will not change very much. Then when the Sun sets there will be a cooling trend but the water will not chill very much before morning. While many people do live near the sea, many do not and the temperature stabilizing effect of the greenhouse gases is of even greater importance to these people.

6.1 Pre-impact World c/w Vapour Canopy

Prior to the arrival of the asteroids and the Great Genesis Flood, the environment of the Earth was much different than it is now. While at the present time the Earth is quite warm near the equator and cold at the poles, during that earlier time the Earth was warm all over. It was warm from pole to pole. Evidence of this warmth in the far north includes the trees of Axel Heiberg Island which is one of the islands of the high Canadian Arctic. Ellesmere Island lies just to the east and goes a little further north and while neither of them go right to the North Pole, at about 83 degrees of latitude the tip of Ellesmere Island is really not very far from the North Pole. The remains of a champsosaur were also found on one of these high arctic islands along with a portion of its once-supportive habitant. The researcher in this case declared that 'wherever a champsosaur could not have been very cold'. Even the Arctic Ocean is declared to have been warm which is far from how it is at the present time. Spitzbergen is another island in the far north and lies almost straight north of Norway. Coal has been found on Spitzbergen and a considerable amount of it has been mined. The plants that form coal do not grow that far north today. In fact very few plants grow on Spitzbergen at all. Similar evidence comes from Antarctica where the remains of tropical trees have been found as well as seams of coal. There is so much evidence available that the assertion that the Polar Regions were once warm is seldom disputed. The phrase 'hot steamy world' has often been used to describe much of the ancient world. It really seems to have been an ideal world to have lived in. Winter coats were never needed.

The problem that presents itself is that in recognition of the heat trapping characteristic of the greenhouse gases, it would have been an impossible situation. This is made clear when we consider the present situation on the Earth. At the present time the areas near the equator are warm and the areas near the poles are cold. The average surface temperature of the Earth is about +15C and with this arrangement a certain amount of water vapour is present in the atmosphere. If we use this as a starting point and then hypothetically increase the temperature at the poles we can see that the ability of the atmosphere to hold more water vapour (than it does at now) would be much increased. This means that the atmosphere would be retaining more heat especially near the Equator because more heat is impinging on these areas. Assuming that the heat from the Sun would have been the same then as it is now, and the greenhouse gases were retaining more heat, the regions near the equator would have been overheated. The temperature around the entire Earth could not have been nearly the same because of the difference in the heat received in different areas. The equatorial regions simply get more heat. If it was warm at the poles, how warm was it at the equator? If it wasn't significantly warmer near the equator than it was near the poles the incoming heat must have been rapidly and continuously distributed from the lower latitudes to the upper latitudes. In fact it must have been distributed more or less equally over the entire surface of the Earth. Some other characteristic of the atmosphere was operating during that ancient time and it was keeping the entire Earth in the warm zone continuously while the equatorial regions were not being overheated.

With the wide range in the amount of incoming heat around the Earth it is difficult to see how the temperature could have been similar all over the Earth without some powerful and continuously-operating heat distribution system. The temperature was not only similar, it was in the comfort zone and well up in the comfort zone at that. This really seems a little too coincidental to have just happened. Was this an Element of Providence?

It is also seriously suspected that in recognition of the apparently prodigious plant growth during that ancient time that CO_2 was present in higher concentrations in the atmosphere. (In fact higher concentrations could possibly partially explain the gigantism of the ancient world as well.) If this was the case it would only have aggravated the situation further because, as a greenhouse gas, CO_2 would also have trapped more heat.

In order for the equatorial regions to be kept from overheating, even though they were receiving more heat is for some of that heat to have been interrupted before it reached the surface of the Earth. It had to have been interrupted high above the surface and then distributed to regions to the north and south. A region of water vapour above the present nitrogen-oxygen atmosphere could have provided an improved heat transfer characteristic as well as a means to interrupt some of the incoming heat so that surface temperatures remained reasonable. A layer of water vapour enveloping the entire planet would have fulfilled these requirements. With a significant portion of the incoming heat interrupted and trapped high up in the atmosphere, the amount reaching the surface would have been much reduced. Therefore, the greenhouse gases could have trapped more of the heat that got through without causing overheating.

There is also independent evidence that a vapour canopy was in place. Oxygen pressure was greater in the past. This has been determined from the analysis of the remains of small ancient creatures. In fact it was concluded that atmospheric oxygen pressure was about 35% higher at that time. A layer of water vapour above the atmosphere equivalent to about ten feet of liquid water could have provided the extra pressure. Just having 35% more oxygen would not have met the requirement for 35% more oxygen pressure because we would also need 35% more nitrogen as well. In other words, It would have required 35% more atmosphere to cause 35% more oxygen pressure. However with this approach it is difficult to imagine how such a large amount of atmosphere could have disappeared. Where did it go? On the other hand disposing of a layer of water vapour could have been readily achieved if it had been seriously disturbed. There is no doubt that an incoming asteroid would have disturbed it and any layer of water vapour that had existed before its arrival, would have precipitated out.

This reality gives us cause to stop and ponder again the idea that the asteroids have arrived at the Earth over widely time-spaced intervals. The very first asteroid to arrive would have demolished any layer of water vapour above the oxygen-nitrogen atmosphere thereby causing the Earth to chill. However the cloud that would have been generated when that first asteroid landed would also have sent the Earth into a world-wide chill. This double-barreled chill factor would have caused the temperature of the Earth to plummet until it was well below freezing. This, in turn, would have caused any water vapour in the oxygen-nitrogen portion of the atmosphere to precipitate out. The greenhouse gas effect of that atmospheric water vapour would have been lost which would only have caused more chilling. The overall result of all of this chilling would have been an Earth that was frozen solid! However there are even more chill factors and hence difficulties involved. Since the first asteroid is expected to have arrived a very long time ago, the heat from the Sun at that time would have been at a much lower level. Current theories of nuclear physics inform us that the heat output from the Sun would have been twenty or twenty-five percent lower at that time than it is at the present time. With such a low heat output the temperature of the Earth would already have been below freezing and there would not have been any atmospheric water vapour anyway. Now we have a great dilemma because we do not have a consistent theoretical situation at all. Some aspect of this whole story must be set aside before any consistency might develop. The likeliest suspect is the idea that the Earth is five billion years old. With our current understanding of how the greenhouse gases influence our climate, the idea that our world is so very old cannot be supported because the Sun would have been too cold. On the other hand, the idea that the asteroids came as a shower provides the basis for a consistent approach with full recognition of the greenhouse gas reality.

There are several ways that the passage of a large asteroid through the atmosphere would have been detrimental to a layer of water vapour in the region above the oxygen-nitrogen layer. It must be recalled, after all, that water vapour is relatively easy to disturb because it is not like many other gases which could have survived the passage of an asteroid with only a transient upset. In these cases, soon after it would have passed, everything would return to normal and there would not be any residual effect. Water, on the other hand can exist in any one of three states – solid, liquid or gas. Further, it is relatively easily changed from one state to another. A layer of water vapour could have disappeared completely if it changed to a liquid. Compression could do this. If the water vapour layer had changed from a gas to a liquid due to being temporarily compressed, it would have simply fallen down as rain. We recall at this point that the report states that it 'rained for forty days and forty nights'. This is not meaningless poetry. A month-long rain is exactly what we would expect if a layer of water vapour above the atmosphere had been disturbed by the passage of a large asteroid.

If an asteroid passed through the atmosphere it would generate a shockwave. This shockwave would move outward with a narrow expanding region of very high pressure. If this happened to most gases they would simply compress, heat up and then decompress and cool down immediately after the high pressure region of the shockwave had passed. As a gas, water vapour would compress all right but compression would cause a change of state into a liquid. As a liquid it would not necessarily be compressed at all so when the high pressure region passed it would just stay as a liquid. A liquid however will not remain in the atmosphere but will just drop out. This would, in effect, wipe out the water vapour layer and it would just disappear. The second mechanism that would spell doom for any layer of water vapour would result from displacement activity. Ifan asteroid happened to rush through the atmosphere, a partial vacuum would develop behind it. Surrounding air would rush into this partial vacuum and follow it all the way to the ground. Since air would now be moving vertically downward, surrounding air would close in behind. At the same time some of the air in front would be moving aside. Thereby a loop would form where air would be moving outward from in front of the asteroid, upward and then in behind the asteroid. All in all there would an overwhelming disturbance to the atmosphere. The rushing air that moved in to follow the asteroid down would have no place to go when the asteroid reached the surface. Therefore by its own momentum it would spread outwards enhancing the circular movement already set up. Since a large asteroid could be five or even ten miles in diameter, it can readily be seen that the outward movement of air along the surface of the Earth would involve several miles. Actually, it could involve several hundred miles and near ground zero this air could have very high speeds and therefore be totally detrimental to any type of animal. Animals would just be bowled over and swept away for miles. From these two factors alone the passage of an asteroid through the atmosphere would have been a total disaster for any layer of water vapour above the oxygen-nitrogen layer. Of course if it had been an asteroid shower, the entire world would have been affected. The entire vapour layer would have fallen out as rain. A world-wide flood would result and if the vapour layer had represented more than just a few inches of liquid water, survival on the surface of the ground would have been very difficult.

While the presence of an envelope of water vapour explains the lack of disparity in the temperature around the world it also helps to explain why it rained for 'forty days and forty nights'. A torrential rain (i.e. gesem rain in the Hebrew) lasting that long could have happened because of a layer of water high above the Earth. Also if it was the cause of 35% greater oxygen pressure, there would have been the equivalent of a layer of water amounting to about ten feet in depth. During the present time the closest we can come to rain of that intensity is during a hurricane. Some hurricanes deposit three feet of water within a couple of days and a few have deposited even more. An ancient flood due to a collapsing vapour canopy would have been like three or four hurricanes raining down on the entire Earth. This factor alone would have constituted a world-wide flood which would not have been survivable.

Prior to the arrival of the asteroid shower the entire Earth was habitable and the surface temperature was in the upper part of the comfort zone. Incoming solar energy was distributed around the entire surface of the Earth in such a way that it was quite comfortable everywhere. The Earth was enveloped in a layer of water vapour (i.e. the waters above the firmament) which not only provided warmth but it also provided protection from ultraviolet light (because ultraviolet light is absorbed by water). In this manner this portion of the incoming solar energy was also useful as heat instead of being destructive of living tissue. The water vapour layer was therefore beneficial to life on the Earth in several ways. Was this most fortuitous arrangement an Element of Providence?

6.2   Impact Period

During the Impact Period, the atmosphere was totally upset just like every other aspect of our environment. Every impact would have produced an immense cloud that would have risen until it was very high up in the atmosphere and then it would have spread out and covered the entire world. Hundreds of volcanoes erupted and each one produced a cloud that would have risen upwards as well before drifting downwind. Some of these volcanic clouds would have spread out and covered significant areas of the Earth's surface all on their own. This would have been similar to the clouds produced by large volcanoes in the Far East during the early eighteen hundreds. In particular, the one named Tambora is said to have produced some thirty-five cubic miles of dust. There are about ten thousand volcanoes around the world and one can only shudder at the idea that the simultaneous eruption of any small percentage of them would have been enough to cause starvation for the whole world without any contribution from the impact clouds at all.

Then, before the clouds even had time to complete their particular form of upset, the ocean started to boil. At least it would have boiled in numerous places with the result that the lower atmosphere would have become completely saturated with water vapour. It would have been so saturated that rain and snow would have started falling almost as soon as the vapour left the surface of the ocean. There was a massive over-supply of water vapour.

The arrival of each individual asteroid would have locally upset the atmosphere from top to bottom and while the effect of its arrival could be called local, local in this case would involve several thousand square miles. Since more than one hundred asteroids landed instead of just one, the entire Earth received an over-supply of upset.

Then the waves started coming. Every asteroid would have generated a train of monster waves and some of these would have had initial heights of several miles. To suggest that some would have started off more than five miles high is not exaggerating in the least. Mount Everest is about six miles high and the atmosphere at the top of Mount Everest is very thin. The bulk of our atmosphere is below the peak of Mount Everest which means that some of the waves produced would have literally been higher than the atmosphere! How would birds have dealt with such disaster?

From the very beginning of the entire affair great waves swept right across the continents and there were many of them. While the impact of an asteroid on water will produce a monster primary wave, it will also produce numerous lesser waves. Even many of these would have been serious business and some of them would also have been able to cross right over continents. An impact directly on a continent would have produced a different wave pattern as the vibrating land all along every coastline would have generated a series of tsunamis for as long as the ground shook. It would have shaken violently for the first few hours before settling down somewhat. It might have kept shaking for days because the magnitude of an asteroid impact is so great that even a single hit on one continent could have caused other continents to shake as well. In recognition of the great energy level (only 1% of the energy of a large asteroid would be sufficient to raise an entire mountain range) of a single speeding asteroid, it would not have been a surprise if all of the continents around the Earth shook in response to several of the largest. In one way or another, the entire world would have been shaking. The third type of wave producer would have developed at some of the antipodes. An antipode is that region of the Earth which is almost directly on the opposite side of the world from an impact. As an asteroid smashes through the crust on one side of the world, it would generate a shockwave which would travel all the way through the interior of the Earth and come up under the crust on the far side. There the crust would surge upwards creating chaotic terrain for miles around when it settled back down again. In some of these cases, the crust would have fractured like a dry cracker and the bedrock of the Earth would have cracked and split leaving behind escarpments, sharp-sided valleys, places where molten material oozed to the surface and places where the bedrock split wide open and didn't quite close up again. An example of millions of square miles of broken bedrock is the Laurentian Plateau of Canada. Here the total disruption is obvious with every kind of rock formation that anyone can imagine. On the positive side it has resulted in excellent resort country with innumerable lakes and rivers. However it is a difficult place to build roads. Once they are built they are quite reliable because the rock that is removed to form a rood pathway is usually crushed for the roadbeds. The Laurentian Plateau extends over three-quarters of Canada and also includes upper New York State, Greenland, and the high Arctic Islands. The rock in this area would have surged upwards for several miles as it was being pushed by a pressure wave from underneath. If anything similar had happened in the ocean the upsurge would have caused the water to start flowing away from the center of the upheaval and flow outwards in all directions. The resulting sheet flow would have shaved the tops right of off any underwater volcanic formations and caused them to have flat tops. The depths of these water-flows would have been hundreds of feet or even thousands. There is no reason to expect that they would have stopped at the continental margins but in some cases would have been powerful enough to wash right over continents just as many of the other waves were doing as well. The force of the upheaval causing the Laurentian Plateau can be somewhat appreciated by noting the magnitude of a structure in the middle of North America called the Mid-Continent Rift. Here, bedrock has been fractured and heaved upwards leaving a split in the Earth more than ten miles deep. In this case the split did not completely reclose with Lake Superior as the result. This rift has partially filled in (probably from material entrained in some of the over-continent water flows) so that Lake Superior is only about six hundred feet deep. In other places the fissure has been filled in right to the top. In particular, the width of this fissure where it crosses Iowa is about fifty percent of the width of the State but on the surface it isn't visible at all.

As the broken bedrock surged upwards it would have interfered with the atmosphere just as the waves did when they surged upwards – in some cases right through the tropopause and into the stratosphere. Mars does not have an atmosphere of any account so when the material on its chaotic side surged upwards any atmospheric disturbance would not have mattered. However, it certainly would have mattered on Earth. The freshly-exposed rock surfaces would have quickly absorbed CO_2, a major greenhouse gas. As the CO_2 inventory dropped so would the atmosphere's ability to retain heat. This loss of an important greenhouse gas would have augmented any cooling trend caused by other factors.

It would have been serious enough if the entire event had only lasted for a couple of days but it lasted much longer than that. It lasted for about five months. The Bible teaches that the water prevailed over the land for one hundred and fifty days. The asteroids kept landing, the waves kept coming and the bedrock kept breaking for five months. At the end of that time the water 'returned from off the land continually'. The continent-dominating phase of the flood was over at that time and things now had a chance to settle down. Settling down would also have required several months. While the vast bulk of the asteroids would have already landed, the Earth would have still been shaking here and there and even a 'little' shake of a few feet would have sent lesser tsunamis out across the ocean once again. There has never been an explanation how anything survived all of this abuse and it isn't even clear how an explanation could be offered. This much trauma is more than a human psyche can handle just as the dropping of the atomic bomb on Japan at the end of World War II was too much for the Japanese psyche to handle.

6.3 Ice Age Period

The darkness over the land produced a chill over the land. Snow started falling even before the last asteroid even landed and before the last continent-crossing wave passed through. As long as the waves over-ran the land, snow could not accumulate on the ground. However within hours after the water drained back into the ocean, the ground froze and the falling snow reached the ground and started to accumulate. Since the ocean was being heated by hot material from the interior surging and oozing to the surface, the evaporation rate of the ocean climbed very steeply. Great banks of moisture drifted over the chilled land and snow fell so fast that even if a person had been standing upright they would have been buried within a few hours. The snow fell heavily right across the northern half of North America, Europe and Asia. The depth of this snow increased until there was so much of it that its own weight pressed it down into ice. It requires about eighty feet of snow to just start to form ice but the snow did not stop at the eighty foot depth. It just kept falling until in some places ten thousand feet of ice accumulated. At a - ice ratio of twelve to one, this would have required about one hundred and twenty thousand feet of snow. This is so much snow that it just boggles the mind thinking about it. If the glaciers that formed on North America, Europe and Asia became as thick as those on Greenland and Antarctica, a similar amount of snow must have fallen on these areas as well. Even if the ice accumulation in these areas was only one mile deep, it would still require about sixty thousand feet of snow. Further, all of it had to fall before the ocean cooled, the clouds broke up and the Sun started shining again.

Of course the cloud cover and the snow build-up were directly related. As the ocean cooled and its evaporation rate subsided, continuous cloud cover would not have been maintained. However it would have taken years to cool the ocean and prodigious quantities of snow would have kept falling right through at least the early phase of cooling. How did the Ark deal with huge quantities of falling snow? Even within the year that the Ark floated, several hundred feet of snow would have fallen across the areas where it eventually accumulated to several thousand feet. If this much had fallen on the Ark, it would have sunk. Was it in a region away from the cooling ocean where great quantities of snow did not fall? Was the area where it landed free of snow as well? If the Ark had landed where there was even one hundred feet of snow, there would have been no hope at all for its cargo. Was the limited amount of snow on both the Ark and the landing area the direct result of involvement of the Deity? Was this an Element of Providence?

6.4 Climate Transition Period

Prior to the arrival of the asteroids, the Earth enjoyed temperatures in the comfort zone over its entire surface. This lies in stark contrast with the current situation where it is cold at both poles and warm at the equator. This means that there must have been a climate transition period when the temperatures around the world were readjusting towards the present arrangement. At that ancient time it is also understood that the ocean was warm. It was warm at the North Pole. It is certainly not warm at the North Pole at the present time so there must have been a cooling down period. In fact, the cooling down would have involved the entire ocean and not just the Arctic Ocean because at the present time the entire ocean is cold. The only warm regions are near the equator at the surface. Even in these areas, within a relatively few meters of the surface the water is noticeably colder and after descending for a few hundred meters, it is very cold. This means in turn that virtually the entire ocean was involved in the cooling down phase.

If the ancient ocean was warm it is appropriate to assume that it was warm from top to bottom. There were three sources of heat for that ancient ocean; the Sun, the atmosphere and the interior of the Earth. Of course the Sun is an obvious source of heat but a warm atmosphere would not have allowed the surface of that ancient ocean to chill. Therefore the surface water would not have been caused to sink to the bottom as it does now. At the present time, currents such as the Gulf Stream, flow northward and gradually cool down. When their water temperature drops to the maximum density point (i.e. about 4C) the water sinks below the surface and drops to the abyss. Circulation continues back toward the equator. Originally this did not happen and surface water just stayed on the surface.

Heat also enters the ocean from the interior of the Earth. Deep in the interior the Earth is hot as can readily be seen when a volcano erupts. Another way that this is evident is under the glaciers of Antarctica. At the ice/rock interface it is warm enough for liquid water to exist. Can anyone imagine liquid water on Antarctica? This even happens relatively close to the South Pole. In some places where the water has pooled into lakes, exploration holes have been opened down to these water reservoirs.

From deep in the interior where it is unquestionably hot, the temperature gradually drops as we move upwards and it continues to decrease until at the ice/rock interface it is near the melting point. The temperature continues to decrease right up to the surface of the ice where it occasionally reaches -100F. However, at the rock/ice interface the temperature is close to 0C over much of the continent. It is the insulating characteristic of the glacial ice that enables this to happen.

The hypothesis that the ocean was originally warm is supported by the existence of the submarine canyons. These underwater canyons, which extend from the mouths of all of the major rivers of the world, would have been formed by the cold melt-water as it left the great ice-fields as the glaciers melted. As it flowed toward the ocean it would not have warmed up very much so when it reached the ocean it would have still been cold and in fact much colder than the ocean which had not yet cooled down that far. Therefore because the ocean was still warm and because warm water is less dense than cold water, it flowed under the surface and headed straight for the bottom. It was enabled to do this simply because the ocean had not yet cooled down. While it would have been cooling relatively rapidly due to evaporation, the cooling cycle would have required several hundred years. During that time the great ice fields were accumulating at a very rapid rate but as the ocean cooled and the evaporation rate reduced the accumulation rate of snow on the ice fields would have slowed down. At first the evaporation rate would have been extraordinarily high because the ocean was not only warm it was warmed further by all of the volcanic activity during the period when the asteroids were pummeling the Earth and breaking its crust. Tons of volcanic material spewed out at that time and very significant levels of volcanic activity would have continued well after the last asteroid struck. From then on the rapid evaporation would have caused the ocean to cool.

Age data from the book of Genesis appears to be tracking the climate transition time period. When this age data is plotted on a graph as shown in the diagrams on the following pages, several patterns become clearly visible. Up until the flood event occurred, a reasonable average life-span can be assigned to the men in the line of descent. A very abrupt change occurs at the time of the flood when life-spans start to be reduced. The reduction however is not a helter-skelter affair but appears to be following a pattern that is very familiar in nature. In fact it is a pattern that is usually followed when something in the natural world changes. It will be noted that the drop-off in life-spans continues right past Moses and that the rate of change also drops off significantly. Life-span reduction can still be identified past Jacob but the slowdown also continues. Neither the change in life-spans nor the drop-off in the rate of change is accidental. It is a certainty that the ancients, including any and all who might have been involved in the record keeping, would not have had any knowledge of this pattern in the change of the life-spans of their ancestors. They were just keeping records. Any understanding of these data could only happen later when the pattern of change was recognized.

Something was happening to cause this particular pattern of change. It appears that some characteristic of nature were changing and that the life-spans were following that change.

The first possibility that comes to mind is that the temperature of the ocean was changing and in fact that it was falling. If it was warm before and it is cold now a great change has taken place. The Age happened during that time. It was absolutely necessary that the ocean evaporate immense quantities of water in order to have the Ice Age. However as the evaporation proceeded the temperature of the ocean would have dropped. During the period when the asteroids were fracturing the crust of the Earth there would have been a great amount of volcanic activity. Once the interior of the Earth was in a turbulent state with shockwaves and pressure surges going back and forth it would probably have taken several years for everything to quiet down. Sooner or later the turbulence in the interior and its manifestation as volcanic activity on the surface would have diminished however and with an accompanying reduction in the release of volcanic heat into the ocean, the temperature of the ocean would have maximized and then started dropping.

The temperature of the ocean is possibly related to the life-span of those ancient human beings through the CO2 link. As water cools it absorbs CO_2 because cold water can hold much more CO_2 than warm water. The level of CO_2 would certainly have dropped due to a drop in ocean temperature. Also, it would have dropped due to freshly-exposed rock. Freshly exposed rock absorbs CO2. CO2 would therefore have been dropping due to two factors and the ongoing drop in ocean temperature means that the level of CO2 in the atmosphere would have continued to drop for years until the temperature of the ocean leveled out at its present level.

There is a possibility that higher levels of CO2 could have been involved in longevity because higher levels of CO2 dilate the blood vessels of an animal allowing more oxygen to penetrate into the brain in greater quantities. This could be the link that relates the change in climate to the change in age. If this was the case it can readily be seen that the age data are tracking the climate transition period. When the ages leveled out at less than one hundred the climate transition period was basically over. All information in the Bible is given for a reason and the changing age data appear to be indicating both the period of the Ice Age and the period of climate transition at the same time.

6.5 Present Climate Period

From a world-wide perspective, our present climate includes very warm temperatures across the lower latitudes on both sides of the equator and bitter cold at the poles. In fact in the immediate vicinity of both poles the temperature seldom rises to the freezing level. It is basically cold all of the time and more so at the South Pole which is far from any moderating influence of the ocean. With such substantial differences in temperature there is major activity involved in transferring heat away from the lower latitudes towards the Polar Regions. The heat transfer medium involves both the atmosphere and the ocean. As the equatorially-heated air moves away from the equator it takes a lot of heat with it. Unfortunately the heat transfer activity includes vertical movement of air in the atmosphere. Storms are the result. Some of these storms develop over a wide area and, due to the Coriolis Effect, the air entrained in the storm rotates. In this manner hurricanes are formed and they commonly spin their destruction for hundreds of miles. Heat is thereby transferred away from the equator.

The other main way that heat leaves the equator is by the ocean water. Great currents have been formed in the ocean and wherever they move to higher latitudes they carry equatorial heat along with them. Heat is transferred for thousands of miles by these mechanisms and if they were not operating there would be even more temperature difference between the low latitudes and the high latitudes.

Generally speaking, these heat transfer mechanisms work for our benefit. As a result the mid-latitudes are quite hospitable to life and the equatorial regions do not become so over-heated that they cannot support animal life at all. Animal activities are more restricted the farther away from the equator we go, but even well above the mid-latitudes life can carry on with the understanding that winter will come and the temperature will be well below the comfort zone for several months every year. Our energy transfer mechanisms contribute to this favourable arrangement and without them only a smaller surface of the Earth would be useable.

The Moon with its consistently repeating orbit has caused the Earth to have seasons. Seasons are not optional, they are absolutely necessary. In order to be habitable, there must be an area which has a frost-free growing season. In addition this area must not get hotter than the temperature at which seeds can germinate (or where body temperature is not exceeded). If the Earth did not have seasons there would only be two bands around the Earth where these criteria could possibly have happened - between about the fortieth latitude and the twenty-fifth latitude. Even this modest allowance might be generous because it would also depend on the atmospheric circulation patterns that would exist. With a cold region and a hot region in such close proximity, there might only be one atmospheric circulation cell instead of the three that we have now. If there was only one, hot air would rise in the tropics, drift north at elevation and then sink when the colder areas were reached. If this was the circulation that would be in place, the return air flow along the surface of the Earth would cause the weather patterns for the narrow 'hospitable' area to come from the north-west in the northern hemisphere. This means that cold air from up north would be sweeping across the possibly-liveable area all year. The result could well be that there really would not be any hospitable area at all. It would be just too cold and the surface temperature might only be hospitable-to-life very close to the tropical region. With this possibility, seasons look more and more attractive and not only attractive but essential for life to exist at all. Since the seasons are caused by the particular mass of the Moon, it's very particular nearly-circular orbit and its very particular distance from the Earth, was this provision an Element of Providence?

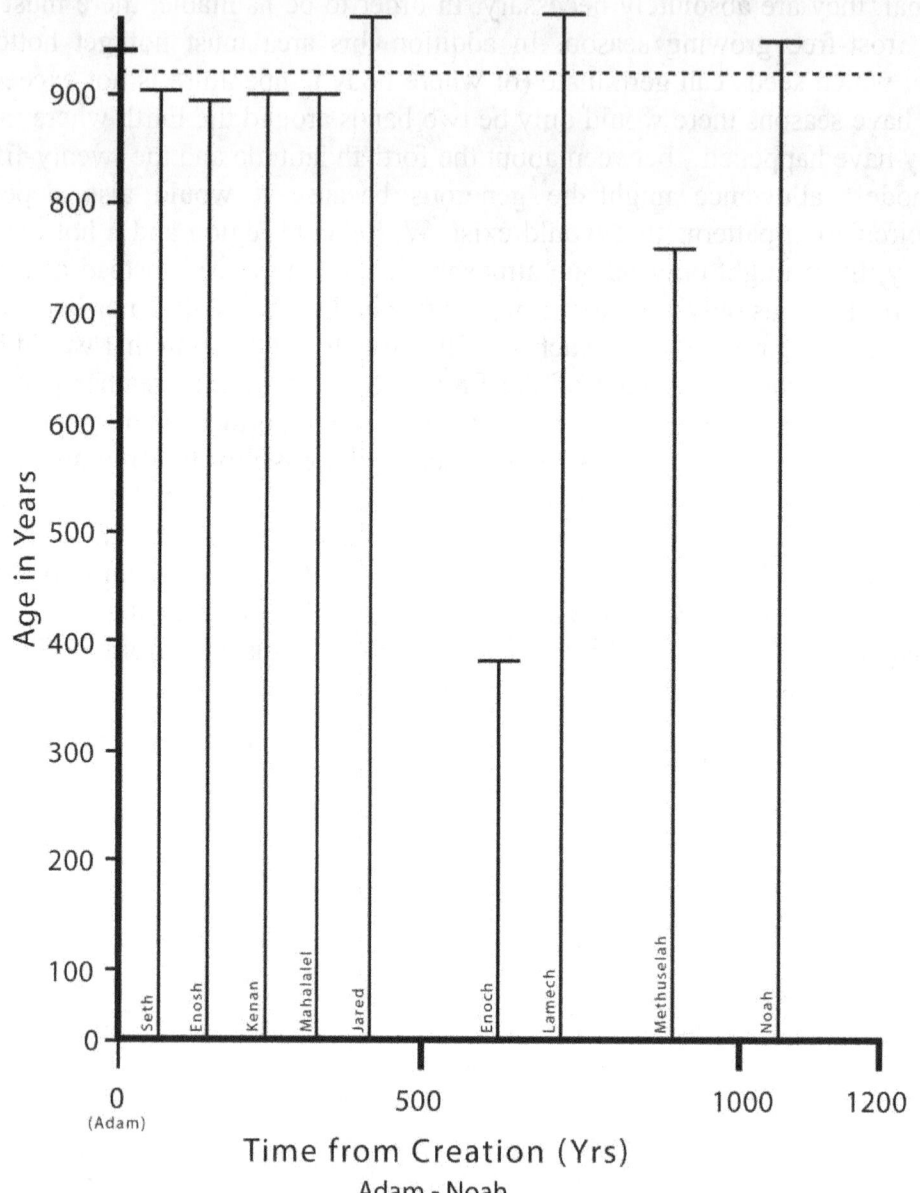

Genesis Life-Span Data
Adam to Noah

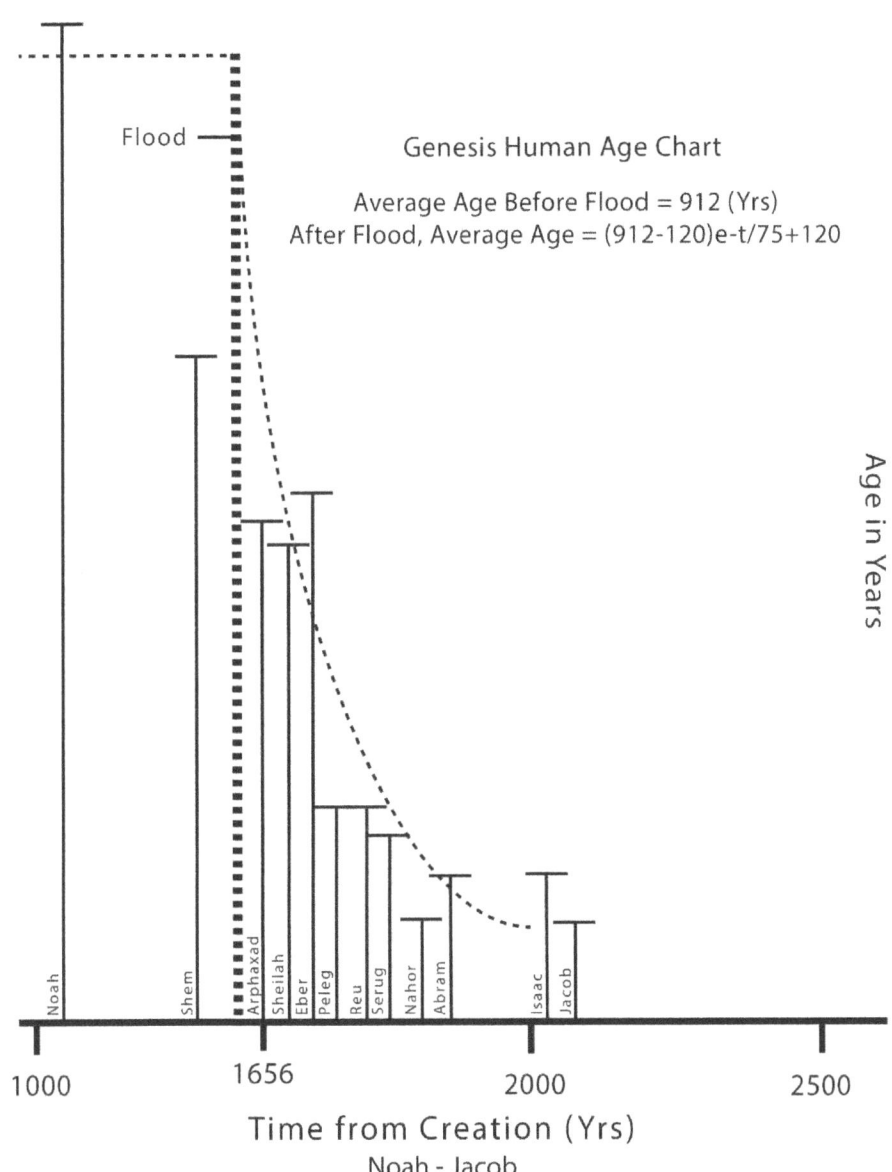

Genesis Life-Span Data
Noah to Jacob

Then, even if a hospitable strip was identified there would be no guarantee that it would persist. Without the stability provided by the orbiting Moon, the orientation of the spinning Earth would drift so that the equator would not necessarily be directly under the Sun at all. It could be anywhere meaning that long-term necessities like forest cover, soil development water storage and distribution as well as the heat transfer mechanisms that currently operate on the Earth would never have time to develop.

What would it be like without any of these energy transfer mechanisms in place or without the seasons or without predictability for the way the Earth rotates? Life on Earth would not be possible.

All of the inhabitants of the Earth also benefit from the Earth having an orbit that is slightly elliptical. It is stretched out slightly from being a perfect circle. This type of orbit brings the Earth in a little closer to the Sun for part of the year and then causes it to be a little further away from the Sun for the other part. It is always the same every year and the orbital bulge does not precess. It does not work its way around. The Earth is always the same distance from the Sun at the same time of the year. Mercury does not have this arrangement and its highly elliptical orbit precesses so that the greater distance from the Sun keeps occurring at different times during the year. Mercury's orbit is not at all repeatable. The orbit of the Earth is always repeated. In addition, the varying distance from the Sun fits together exactly with the Earth's angle of inclination to provide optimal heating for the entire Earth all year. During summer in the northern hemisphere the Earth is a little further from the Sun. In this manner the northern hemisphere tends not to over-heat whereas if it was closer to the Sun at that time it would over-heat. Similarly during winter in the northern hemisphere the Earth is a little closer to the Sun and we do not get quite as cold as we would otherwise. While the Earth's orbit is only slightly elliptical, (i.e. non-circular) it is exactly the right amount. The Earth's axis of inclination and its elliptical orbit work synergistically to provide optimal heating conditions. How could such an advantageous arrangement ever have happened? How could this ever have resulted after the Earth was pummeled repeatedly? Was this an Element of Providence?

6.6 Tranquility to Chaos to Tranquility

Before the arrival of the swarm of asteroids it seems that the climate of the Earth was close to being ideal for life from pole to pole. This implies that the greenhouse gas temperature stability factor was working properly and that the orbit of the Earth around the Sun was right where it needed to be for optimal benefit. Then without warning, incomprehensible chaos struck and continued for months.

The evidence of chaos around the world is well summarized by Immanuel Velikovsky in his book entitled; Earth in Upheaval, wherein there is an excellent description of what would happen on Earth if it was struck by one or more large asteroids. Velikovsky states; 'Whenever we investigate the geological and paleontological records of this earth we find signs of catastrophes and upheavals, old and recent. Mountains sprang from plains, and other mountains were leveled; strata of the terrestrial crust were folded and pressed together and overturned and moved and put on top of other formations; igneous rock melted and flooded enormous areas of land with miles-thick sheets; the ocean bed flowed with molten rock; ashes showered down and built layers many yards thick on the ground and on the bottom of the oceans in their vast expanse; shores of ancient lakes were tilted and are no longer horizontal; seacoasts show subsidence or emergence, in some places over one thousand feet; rocks of the earth are filled with remains of life extinguished in a state of agony; sedimentary rocks are one vast graveyard, and the granite and basalt, too, have embedded in them numberless living organisms; and shells have closed valves as they do in a living state, so unexpectedly came the entombment; and vast forests were burned and washed away and covered with the waters of the seas and with sand and turned to coal; and animals were swept to the far north and thrown into heaps and were soaked by bituminous outpourings; and broken bones and torn ligaments and the skins of animals of living species and of extinct were smashed together with splintered forests into huge piles; and whales were cast out of the oceans onto mountains; and rocks from disintegrating mountain ridges were carried over vast stretches of land, from Norway to the Carpathians, and into the Harz Mountains, and into Scotland, and from Mount Blanc to the Juras, and from Labrador to the Poconos; and the Rocky Mountains moved many leagues from their place, and the Alps traveled a hundred miles northward, and the Himalayas and the Andes climbed ever higher; and the mountain lakes emptied themselves over barriers, and continents were torn by rifts, and the sea bottom by canyons; and land disappeared under the sea, and the sea pushed new islands from its bottom, and sea beds were turned into high mountains bearing sea shells, and shoals of fish were poisoned and boiled in the seas, and numberless rivers lost their channels, were dammed by lava and turned upstream, and the climate suddenly changed; tillable land and meadows turned into vast deserts. Reindeer from Lapland and polar fox and arctic bears from the snowy tundras and rhinoceroses and hippopotami from the African jungles, and lions from the desert and ostriches, and seals, were thrown into piles and covered with gravel, clay, and tuff, and the fissures of multitudes of rocks are filled with broken bones; regions where the palm grew were moved into the Arctic, and oceans steamed, and the evaporated seas condensed under clouds of dust and built mountainous covers of ice over great stretches of continents, and the ice melted on heated ground and cast icebergs into the oceans in enormous fleets; and all volcanoes erupted, and all human dwellings were shattered and burned, and animals tame and fierce and human beings with them ran for refuge to mountain caves, and mountains swallowed and entombed those that reached the refuge, and many species and genera and families of the animal kingdom were annihilated down to the very last one; and the earth and the sea and the sky again and again united their elements in one great work of destruction.' (This quotation has been copied from 'Earth in Upheaval' by Immanuel Velikovsky as published by Random House Publishers in 1955 and used here with the kind permission of Rafael Sharon, his grandson)

The ocean over-ran the land. Any material that was moveable on the land, moved. Massive quantities of gravel were relocated. Great quantities of silt that would soon harden into sedimentary rock were swept away and laid in great layers one on top of another. Massive quantities of vegetable matter were rolled and tumbled along until they lodged in some recess or until the force of the moving water diminished too much and they just stalled. Soon another sheet of crashing water appeared with a load of silt and covered these great masses which later became coal. The magnitude of the chaos was indescribable. In some places the crust of the Earth was thrust upwards for thousands of feet (over thousands of square miles) and fractured. Escarpments and mountains were formed. Great fissures in the crust of the Earth were formed. The sky went completely dark and stayed dark for months. Hurricane rain drenched the Earth with a layer of water averaging several feet deep over the entire surface of the Earth. The land became cold. It snowed and it snowed a lot. It some places it snowed 10,000 feet of snow. Then, later, the snow melted. This wasn't really much of an improvement for a while because it melted so fast that every river overflowed its banks as it surged to the sea. Since the sea had not yet cooled down, the great flows of cold melt-water went straight to the bottom forming submarine canyons. Things gradually quieted down. Then the Sun shone through the clouds. It was later realized that we somehow wound up with a Goldilock's orbit and a complement of greenhouse gases that regulated the Earth's temperature and kept it right at the optimum level. How could all of this have happened? It must have been near an optimum level before all of the upset and somehow obtained another optimum level after all of the trauma had subsided. And somehow through the entire affair a remnant of life was able to survive. There isn't any logical explanation for any of this. Was there a thread of the Supernatural throughout the entire affair? Was this an Element of Providence?

6.7 Provision of Hot-Cold Balance

By the time the ocean cooled and lost its ability to produce water vapour for the greenhouse gas effect, Ice Age maximum had been passed and the cold resulting from the cloud-cover induced chill had diminished. There was an appropriate balance between water vapour production and cloud-cover cooling. Otherwise the greenhouse gas temperature-stabilizing factor would have been lost. This balance must have continued throughout the entire affair. Was this an Element of Providence?

7. Beringia, an Ice Age Fairy Tale

There is currently a belief, widely accepted, even among Bible-believing Christians, that a certain group of very large mammals survived the Ice Age. The essence of this belief has even been captured in various articles one of which was entitled; 'Beringia, an Ice Age Serengeti'. The Serengeti is a region in Africa where numerous animals roam freely over many square miles of African grassland. Since the region supports a large number of animals, it is considered to be about as close as we can get to an ideal environment for the large creatures that live there.

Beringia, on the other hand, is far from Africa and far from a warm climate. It is actually a fairly loose term referring to western Alaska, eastern Russia and the bottom of the ocean in between these two areas as well as ocean bottom to the north and south. It includes all of the ocean bottom which would have been exposed at Ice Age maximum which includes areas of the ocean that are currently less than about 400 feet deep. When this area of ocean bottom was exposed it was thought to have grown grass. In fact it was thought to have grown grass in abundance to feed large animals like the Woolly Mammoth. All of this grass-growing and animal feeding is declared to have carried on right through the Flood and the Ice Age. National Geographic identifies the area as having an abundance of 'nutrient-rich grass'. The animals were to have accessed this grass by pawing through the snow. This, at first, appears as a possibly-credible scenario – partly because of the publisher – to explain how the animals survived. To their credit, when one offers a theory of any sort it is quite appropriate to explain how it happened. In this case the animals survived by eating the grass under the snow. However these activities would have had to carry on right through the world-wide flood and the Ice Age as well as all of the other woes brought about by the impacting asteroids. The currently-available evidence of 'fresh' ivory from northern Russia, directly contradicts the idea that anything survived. The animals involved not only did not survive, they were swept away in such a violent manner that their tusks were broken off. How hard would it have been to break the tusk off of a large animal like a woolly mammoth? The impulse from a hammer would not have been able to do it. Even being knocked down would not have been enough. The animal must have been tumbled repeatedly in a violent manner for this to have happened. The great Woolly Mammoths did not survive the asteroid-impact, world-wide flood, Ice-Age event at all. They died (and were swept away into great heaps) like every other land-based animal died, just as the Genesis report insists.

8. Review

A partial list of the woes that would have accompanied many of the more than one hundred impacts that the Earth has endured, is appropriately discussed here starting with the blinding flash. As a high-speed asteroid approaches contact with the Earth, the air in front of it becomes compressed and so hot that it will glow white hot. This happens simply because the air cannot move off to the side fast enough to allow the asteroid to pass through. There would actually be a temporary hole in the atmosphere extending behind the asteroid's pathway and the air that had been in that space a fraction of a second earlier would now be caught around in front of the speeding asteroid. Much of it would simply compress. A powerful pulse of light would result from the temperature increase. This pulse would be intensive enough to ignite forests and grasslands and anything else that was combustible out for possibly several hundred miles all around. Of course any animals caught in the area would be instantly set ablaze. The flash would be similar to what happens when a nuclear bomb is exploded. There was a case reported from World War II in Japan of a horse that was reasonably close to ground zero. The flash set the horse on fire and its skin on one side burned right off. Woolly Mammoths or any other animal would not have survived any better. Of course some of the air in the path of the asteroid would slip off to the side and form a region of highly compressed air. This tube of air would have been given an outward push and would become an expanding shockwave which would also propagate out across the country-side after the blinding flash. Unfortunately this pressure wave would not be limited to a line-of-site pathway and would be very destructive for several thousand miles. Trees and animals would simply be blown away by the expanding wall of doom which would have been similar to an expanding plate of steel.

Something similar happened during the Tunguska event in central Siberia in 1908. The pressure wave from the exploding asteroid (or Comet) flattened the trees outward from ground zero for about 30 miles in all directions. No animal could have survived that event either.

The pressure wave would hardly have passed before the earthquake would have showed up. This would have been a special kind of earthquake where the land heaves up and down as well as back and forth. Some commentators have offered that the crust of the Earth would heave up and down by one thousand feet one thousand miles from ground zero. Unfortunately the ground would also be heaving back and forth at the same time. It would in fact move out from under any animal and move laterally so fast that the animal would be left nearly in the same position. Just to make it worse when the land was ascending the g forces would flatten it and immediately the land would have descended and the animal would hardly have been able to stay on the ground. This would have been much worse than descending in a mine elevator which can drop so fast that a passenger's weight is temporarily reduced. While the atmospheric shockwave would pass, the earthquake would not pass and the ground would keep vibrating for some time – possibly all day or even all week. Next, the first tsunami would arrive. It could have been generated by the earthquake or by an asteroid impacting directly on the ocean. This would not really matter because in either case it would still be moving close to tsunami speed which speeds are usually comparable to the speeds of a jet plane. Further, these great waves would not be singular but might number more than one hundred from a single impact. Some of them would be moving at a significant fraction of the speed of sound and they would, in all likelihood, have been audible. There would not only have been moving water but entrained within the water there would have been all manner of debris including trees and gravel. The moving water would sweep away the soil and reposition it some distance away while bringing other material to leave behind. If there had been any Woolly Mammoths present they would have been alarmed at the great crashing sound of the water but they probably would not have seen it coming because the impact of the asteroid would also have generated a cloud which would have risen at least to the tropopause and then spread out in all directions. This cloud would have been so massive that it would have blocked the Sun from most of the Earth causing a type of darkness which would make it impossible to see anything at all. It would have been similar to being in a coal mine with the lights off. The next hazard would materialize because of this darkness which would have caused it to become cold. The temperature would drop to below freezing within a few hours of impact. Any plant life that was left would freeze. Surface freezing would be delayed until the waves stopped coming because the waves would have been composed of warm water. As soon as they stopped rolling through however everything would freeze. Now what is our Woolly Mammoth going to eat? Also what is it going to breathe? A large number of volcanoes would have erupted because of the asteroid and the air would be full of chocking dust and undesirable aerosols. Within a few weeks after the last asteroid landed, the waves would stop coming but now the snow would be falling. The Ice Age would have begun. A lot of snow fell during the Ice Age and in some places more than one hundred thousand feet of it fell. The question must be asked again. Where will our Woolly Mammoth take shelter, under the snow? There is simply no credible scenario for the survival of any animal following the arrival of a single asteroid let alone a shower of asteroids. To suggest that large animals pawed through the snow is completely absurd. There has never been an animal that could survive in one thousand feet of snow and it is not very likely that one will ever be found. The Woolly Mammoths all died. Many would have died from the atmospheric shockwave. In fact there is evidence to suggest this mode of death quite clearly. The food that they were eating was still in their mouths. They were swept away and deposited in great piles. Their blood vessels were ruptured inside of their skin and the blood was full of oxygen. This means that death came suddenly and it was not by suffocation. The entire herd died the same hour and their tusks were broken off as they were tumbled to their final resting places. There is no way that any animal could have survived any of these miseries and no way that any one of them could have survived the collective misery of the entire event! To suggest that there was a Serengeti-like life-supporting environment during the Great Ice Age is totally unrealistic.

The notion that an ice age developed because the Earth chilled is also very widely accepted at the present time. 'A chilled Earth equals an Earth having an ice age', is not only invalid it is bizarre! There are two main reasons why the idea is incorrect. Firstly, when water becomes chilled, it will not evaporate. It requires heat to evaporate water and without a supply of heat it will remain in a liquid state. In fact the amount of heat that is required to evaporate water is quite high – even after its temperature has been raised right up to the boiling point. Of course water will evaporate to some degree whenever its temperature is between melting and boiling but it always requires the same amount of heat to evaporate any particular volume of it and the required amount is quite high. While less-than-boiling water will evaporate it will cool itself down in the process. Then when it is cooler and evaporates a little more it will cool down a little more. This is the exact opposite of what is required to evaporate large amounts of water. In general heat must be continually added to water to keep it evaporating. If heat is not added and some water evaporates pretty soon the temperature of the remaining water will approach the freezing point. Even right at the freezing point some water will still evaporate because the vapour pressure of the liquid water is still slightly positive. Then of course if the water chills a little more, it will freeze. Therefore it can be properly concluded that if the Earth suffered an overall chill, soon the oceans would be chilled and they would crust over with a layer of ice. When this happens there would not be any evaporation at all. Without moisture being released into the air, there would not be any moisture to fall as snow. Consequently there would not be any snowfall and certainly not any build up of snow without which there would certainly not be an ice age. Even at the present time when the oceans of the world are not covered by a layer of ice but in fact are several degrees above freezing in most places there isn't any overall build up of snow and ice occurring. On the other hand the Ice Age required such an unthinkably large volume of snow to fall that it staggers the imagination to imagine how it could have happened at all. A valid corollary could be drawn at this point to conclude that an ice age would be a very rare event and it would be a surprise that it could happen at all. To think that it could have happened repeatedly is to avoid recognition of the immensity of the quantity of heat that every one of the repeat ice ages would have required in order to happen. Suggesting that every few thousand years another ice Age developed can only be proposed if basic physics is completely ignored.

Then to make matters even worse for the proponents of a multiple ice age scenario we must recognize the nature of our greenhouse gases. Those parts of the atmosphere that are referred to as greenhouse gases are an absolutely essential component of the Earth's temperature regulation system and without the temperature controlling characteristic that they provide there would not be any life on Earth at all. We recall that the two main components in the Earth's heat supply are the energy from the Sun and the greenhouse gases. Both are needed in the right amount and the right combination to keep the average surface temperature of the Earth right where it is at approximately +15C. If an overall chill were introduced as it would be with 'a chilled Earth is an Earth having an ice age' offering, the temperature would spiral right on down as more and more water vapour was lost from the air. If we chill the Earth slightly we lose some of our water vapour. This would cause the Earth to chill a little bit more and so on until a state was reached where any farther chilling would not result in any further reduction in the water vapour content in the air. Unfortunately this would not happen until the temperature was below freezing. If the Earth ever became chilled a little too much on a global basis the temperature would start spiraling down and continue to spiral down until the surface layers of the Earth became frozen solid. This would be the result if the Earth should drift a little too far from the Sun or if it somehow drifted into a region of space where the heat from the Sun was diminished. The idea that 'a chilled Earth is an Earth having an ice age' is not a valid concept.

The Ice Age would certainly have disrupted the temperature of the Earth. Some effects of the Ice Age were very wide-spread and claims have even been made that the entire surface of the Earth was involved. This is admittedly a serious claim but it is realistic when it is recalled that the asteroid shower – or even a single major hit – would have produced a layer of cloud that would have completely blocked the Sun for months. The entire Earth would therefore have chilled. This development alone would have been the end of life on the Earth and it actually nearly was the end because a world-wide ice age would not have been survivable especially if it had been caused by an externally-originating world-wide chill.

It is a wonder that the irreversibility of a major chilling effect has not terminated life on Earth as a result of much more recent happenings. In the early 1800's there was series of major volcanic eruptions in the Far East that produced so much cloud that the overall temperature of the Earth was caused to drop. In North America and Europe food could not be grown and there was widespread famine. While the cloud reduced the average temperature around the entire Earth, it cleared before the temperature of the ocean measurably dropped. Volcanoes were erupting and this always releases a great amount of heat. In this case the heat would have helped to keep the temperature, on a global basis, from dropping. This was possibly the factor that enabled the Earth to escape the deep freeze during that stressful time. It is preferred that this type of situation never repeats. However, fortunately it is quite rare for three major eruptions to happen within a four year period so the likelihood of a repeat is quite low.

In order for the Earth to have avoided the irreversible deep freeze caused by a globe-enveloping cloud is for the same event to release enough heat to offset the cold. The arrival of the asteroids would certainly have resulted in a drop in the world-wide temperature but the volcanic activity – particularly underwater – would have been the offsetting heat factor required. But how can this type of coincidence be explained? 'A great amount of cold is appropriately offset by a great amount of heat' is very difficult to explain. Was this an Element of Providence?

A shower of asteroids would also have modified the orbit of the Earth. The amount of modification can never be known and neither can the aggregate level of the impulse that these impacting asteroids would have brought. The Earth might be hard to move but it isn't constrained by anything other than its own mass. There is really nothing to stop it from being nudged a little if it is hit hard enough. How much would have been too much? The question arises because it seems clear enough that before all of the upset brought by the asteroids, the Earth had an ideal orbit. The entire Earth was warm and a perfectly lovely place to be. It must therefore be concluded that its orbit was in exactly the right location. Then the asteroids struck and the Earth's orbit wound up once again in exactly the right location where-from it cannot be varied by even a small amount or disaster is expected to follow. The present orbit of the Earth acting together with the inclination of the Earth's axis evens out the temperature in an optimal manner. The heat absorbing ocean faces the Sun when we are closer to the Sun and the surface of the Earth with lower specific heat (i.e. the continents)is facing the Sun more at the time of year when the Earth is further away from the Sun. This is another most fortuitous situation. How could such an optimal arrangement have resulted from a major upset? Was this an Element of Providence?

With the Maria and the mass concentrations on one side of the Moon and a bulge and chaotic terrain on the other side it is clear that the Moon has been impacted several times by asteroids. There are, of course, numerous impact marks in addition to the Maria but these particular areas appear to have taken the largest hits. All of the Maria are on one side. The aggregate impulse from all of these impacts would have been expected to change the orbit of the Moon. Since the Moon is not nearly as massive as the Earth the overall effect of the impacts would expectedly have shown up as a change in the Moon's orbit. Why is the Moon's orbit an almost perfect circle? Why is the plane of the Moon's orbit inclined to the plane of the Earth's orbit at exactly the right angle for the Earth to have an optimal seasonal arrangement? The Earth's seasons are as close to ideal as could ever have been arranged. In order for this to be the case, three factors involving the Moon must be in place. The size of the Moon has to be just right. These factors are individually at just the right value and collectively at just the right combination for the very best arrangement that could be envisaged for the Earth. Further, the entire arrangement is in place and operating properly after a swarm of asteroids passed by on their way further into the inner solar system. How could such an improbable combination of factors ever be lined up at any time not counting after a major upset? All of the factors related to the Moon result in a necessary life-enabling characteristic of the Earth's environment tin that they actually enable the Earth to have an optimal seasonal arrangement. The combination of all of these factors is so improbable that it is impossible to explain apart from supernatural design and intervention. Were these developments Elements of Providence?

9. Summary

Due to the tumult of water movement during the first five months of the Flood, the Ark would have been subjected to bending and twisting. It was a very large vessel and it was only made of wood. How was it able to withstand such conditions for such an extended period of time?

The water wasn't just water. It was loaded with all manner of debris including tumbling masses of trees and great quantities of aggregates such as sand and gravel. How did the Ark withstand being impacted by solid material?

It was cold and it was dark. How did the inhabitants of the Ark deal with these factors?

The air was contaminated with volcanic dust and aerosols. Was the air that the Ark's inhabitants breathed filtered somehow?

The world-enveloping cloud together with the volcanic activity caused the world to be both dark and cold. The greenhouse gas temperature stability factor was being threatened. How did the temperature manage to stay within the habitable range?

As the whole event unfolded both a world-wide chill factor and an ocean heating factor developed. The chill was so serious that massive ice-fields ten thousand feet thick were enabled to accumulate. The heating factor was so overwhelming that hundreds and hundreds of feet of ocean water evaporated. How did the average temperature remain in the habitable range?

The Earth was repeatedly pummeled by large speeding masses of rock. There is a possibility that this activity changed the orbit of the Earth. How is it that the Earth currently has an optimal orbit?

The chill brought on by the cloud, which would have persisted for months and even years in some places, would have reduced the quantity of water vapour in the air. Since water vapour is a greenhouse gas, a reduction in water vapour of this nature could have caused the Earth to sink into a sub-freezing state and just stay there. The extensive fracturing of the Earth's crust would have released hot volcanic material into the ocean causing it to boil and release great quantities of water vapour. This would have enabled the water vapour inventory to be replenished. Since both the cloud and the heat in the ocean would have taken many decades to dissipate, how was this done in a balanced way so that many years later an appropriate greenhouse gas inventory resulted?

There are several clear and obvious examples of intervention by the Deity during the Great Flood Event. There are also several examples of situations that appear much too coincidental to have just happened. The arrangement, timing and magnitude of these situations are not readily explained by the world of science and this causes one to seriously stop and ponder. Were these less-than-obvious situations also Elements of Providence just like the more obvious ones?

Biblography

Number	Reference	Abbreviation
1.	A Short History of Nearly Everything, By Bill Bryson, Anchor Canada, a division of Random House of Canada Limited	Short
2.	American Petroleum Geologist Bulletin 56 No 2 1972,	Am Pet1
3.	An Ice Age Caused by the Genesis Flood by Michael J. Oard, Institute for Creation Research, P.O. Box 2667, El Cajon, California 92021	Ice Age
4.	Apocalypse When? Cosmic Catastrophe and the Fate of the Universe by Frank Close William Morrow and Company Inc., New York	Comets
5.	ASHRAE Handbook Fundamentals, American Society of Heating Refrigeration and Air-Conditioning Engineers Inc., 1791 Tullie Circle, NE Atlanta GA 30329	Fun 1981
6.	By Design, By Jonathan Sarfati PhD, Creation Book Publishers, Atlanta Georgia	By Design
7.	Canada from Space, By Brian Banks, Camden House Publishing, Suite 100, 25 Shepherd Ave. West, North York, ON M2N 6S7	Canada
8.	Cassell's Atlas of Evolution, By Andromeda, Weidenfield & Nicolsen, London UK	A of E
9.	Chemistry by James V. Quagliano Prentice – Hall Inc., Englewood Cliffs, New Jersey, USA	Chem
10.	Climate Wars, by Gwynne Dyer, Random House Canada	Climate
11.	College Physics by Weber, White and Manning, McGraw-Hill Book Company, New York NY	College
12.	Comets and Asteroids and Future Cosmological Catastrophes compiled by Glen W. Chapman, www.2s2.com/chapmanresearch	Cosmic
13.	Creation Matters, Creation Research Society, P.O. Box 8263, St. Joseph MO 64508-8263 USA	CM

Number	Reference	Abbreviation
14.	Creation Research Society Quarterly, 6801 N. Hwy 89, Chino Valley AZ 86323	CRSQ
15.	Design and Origins in Astronomy, By George Mulfinger, Jr., Creation Research Society Books	Design
16.	Earth Impact Database, www.unb.ca/passc/Impact Database	EID
17.	Earth in Upheaval by Immanuel Velikovsky, Dell Publishing Co., Inc., 1 Dag Hammarskjold Plaza, New York NY 10017	E in U
18.	Encyclopedia Britannica 1958, Published by William Benton, Chicago London Toronto	En Br
19.	Engineering Mechanics, Dynamics, by Meriam & Kraige, John Wiley & Sons Inc, New York, London	Eng Mech
20.	Field Notes from a Catastrophe, By Elizabeth Kolbert 2007, Bloomsbury, USA	Notes
21.	1st International Conference on Creationism Vol II	Conf 1
22.	Funk & Wagnalls New Encyclopedia, Edited by Robert S. Phillips, Funk and Wagnalls	F & W
23.	Grand Canyon, The Story Behind the Scenery, By Merrill D. Beal, KC Publications Inc., P.O. Box 14883, Las Vegas, Nevada 89114	Grand
24.	Handbook of Chemistry and Physics, 52nd Edition, The Chemical Rubber Publishing Company, 18901 Cranwood Parkway, Cleveland Ohio 44128	Handbook
25.	Historical Geology, By Carl Owen Dunbar, John Wiley & Sons Inc., New York London	Geology
26.	How It Works, The Magazine That feeds Minds	HIW
27.	In the Minds of Men by Ian T. Taylor, TFE Publishing, Toronto	In the Minds
28.	Kronos Press, PO Box 313, Wynnewood PA 19096	Kronos

Number	Reference	Abbreviation
29.	MacLeans, 11th Floor, One Mount Pleasant Road, Toronto, ON M4Y 2Y5, Vol. 122, Number 24, June 29, 2009	Mac1
30.	Macleans, Aug. 14, 2000	Mac3
31.	Macleans, Aug. 24, 2009	Mac2
32.	Modern University Physics, By Richards, Sears, Wehr & Zemansky, Addison-Wesley Publishing Company Inc., Reading Mass., USA	Modern
33.	National Geographic Society, 17th and M Streets, NW Washington DC 20036	Nat Geo
34.	Nature Alberta, By James Cavanagh, Lone Pine Publishing, Edmonton, Alberta	Nature
35.	Pensee, Student Academic Freedom Forum, P.O. Box 414, Portland Oregon 97207	Pensee
36.	Peoples of the Sea, by Immanuel Velikovsky, Doubleday & Company Inc., Garden City, New York	Peoples
37.	Petrified Forest, The Story Behind the Scenery, By Sidney R. Ash and David D. May, Petrified Forest Museum Association, Petrified Forest national Park, Holsbrook Arizona 86025	Pet For
38.	Physiology and Biophysics by Ruch and Patton, Nineteenth edition, W. B. Saunders Company, Philadelphia and Company	P&B
39.	Postcards from Mars, by Jim Bell, Penquin Group (USA), 375 Hudson Street, New York NY 10014	Postcards
40.	Principles of Microbiology Eighth Edition, By Alice Lorraine Smith, The C. V. Mosby Company, 11830 Westline Industrial Drive, Saint Lewis Missouri 63141	Principles
41.	Scientific American Inc., 415 Madison Ave., New York NY	Sci Am
42.	Silent Snow by Marla Cone, Grove Press, 841 Broadway, New York NY 10003	Silent

Number	Reference	Abbreviation
43.	Starlight & Time by D. Russel Humphreys PhD, Master Books Inc., PO Box 726, Green Forest AR 72638	S & T
44.	The Beothucks or Red Indians, By James P. Howley, Prospero Canadian Collection	Beo
45.	The Big Splash, by Dr, Louis A. Frank, Avon Books, New York	Splash
46.	The Concise Oxford Dictionary, edited by H.W. Fowler and F.G. Fowler, Oxford	Oxford at the Clarendon Press
47.	The Concise Oxford Dictionary, Oxford University Press, Walton Street, Oxford, 0X2 6DP	Oxford
48.	The End of the World, by John Leslie, Routledge	The End
49.	The Genesis Flood, by Whitcomb & Morris, The Presbyterian and Reformed Publishing Company, Philadelphia, Pennsylvania, 29 West 35th Street, New York, NY 10001	The Flood
50.	The Greatest Show on Earth, By Richard Dawkins, Free Press, New York	The Greatest
51.	The Living Cosmos by Chris Impey, Random House New York	Living
52.	The Moon Its Creation Form and Significance, By John C. Whitcomb/Donald B. DeYoung, BMH Books, Winona Lake, Indiana 46590	The Moon
53.	The New World of the Oceans, Men and Oceanography, by Daniel Behrman, Little Brown & Company	New
54.	The Oceans, By Sylvia Earle & Ellen Prager, McGraw-Hill Book Company, New York NY	Oceans
55.	The Rough Guide to the Universe by John Scalzi, Rough Guide Ltd., 80 Strand, London, WCR2 ORL	Rough
56.	The Scientific American Book of the Cosmos, Daniel H. Levy Editor, St. Martin's Press, New York, New York	Cosmos

Number	Reference	Abbreviation
57.	The Sea Around Us by Rachel Carson, Oxford University Press Inc. 2003, 198 Madison Ave., New York NY 10016	The Sea
58.	The Sun and Stars, By J C Brandt, 1966, McGraw Hill Book Company, New York NY	The Sun
59.	The Trouble with Physics by Lee Smolin, Houghton Mifflin Company, 215 Park Avenue South, New York, New York 10003	Trouble
60.	The Violent Face of Nature, by Kendrick Frazier, William Morrow and Company Inc., New York 1979	Violent
61.	Time Upside Down, By Erich A. Von Fange, 460 Pine Brae Drive, Ann Arbor MI 48105	Time
62.	Weather, A Visual Guide by Buckley, Hopkins and Whitaker, Firefly Books Ltd. 2008	Weather
63.	Worlds in Collision by Immanuel Velikovsky, Doubleday & Company, Garden City, New York	W in C
64.	In The Hills, published by MonoLog Communications Inc. R. R. 1, Orangeville, ON	

Index

Africa, 34, 35, 69
Ancient
 ancient, 65
Antarctica, 3, 23, 49, 56, 58
Asteroid
 asteroid, i, x, xi, xii, 7, 8, 9, 21, 22, 28, 29, 32, 33, 34, 35, 36, 37, 38, 40, 46, 50, 51, 52, 53, 54, 56, 58, 69, 71, 72, 74
Atmosphere
 atmosphere, xi, 13, 17, 18, 22, 28, 36, 40, 47, 49, 50, 51, 52, 53, 54, 55, 57, 59, 60, 71, 74
Atomic bomb
 atomic bomb, 11, 56
Axel Heiberg, 49
Beringia, 69
blinding flash, 71
Boil
 boil, 24, 53, 77
Bullet
 bullet, 9, 33
Caloris Basin, 40
Canada, 79
Canadian, 49, 82
Carbon dioxide
 carbon dioxide, 13, 18, 47
Champsosaur
 champsosaur, 49
Chaos, 64
 chaos, 65
Chesapeake Bay, 8, 34
Chicxulub, 8, 34
Climate
 climate, 15, 37, 51, 57, 58, 60, 64, 65, 69
Cloud
 cloud, xi, 11, 21, 22, 26, 28, 36, 51, 53, 57, 67, 72, 74, 75, 77
Coal
 coal, 65
Cohort
 cohort, xii, 37

Congo, 34, 35
Coriolis, 60
Dust
 dust, 66
Earth
 earth, 65, 66, 80, 82
Earthquake
 earthquake, 71
Element
 element, 9, 11, 12, 13, 14, 21, 22, 29, 37, 39, 42, 43, 44, 45, 46, 50, 53, 57, 61, 64, 66, 67, 75
Energy
 energy, 7, 8, 18, 19, 23, 26, 31, 32, 33, 34, 35, 40, 54, 61, 64, 74
Epic of Gilgamesh, ix
Erratic
 erratic, 36
Europe, 7, 23, 34, 37, 56, 75
Evidence
 evidence, ix, x, xi, xii, 2, 11, 21, 28, 37, 49, 50, 65, 69, 72
Fish
 fish, 65
Genesis, i, iii, ix, 1, 3, 7, 9, 11, 13, 21, 36, 48, 58, 62, 63, 69, 79, 82
Glaciers
 glaciers, 19, 23, 24, 27, 37, 56, 58
Goldilock's, 45, 46, 66
Grand Canyon, 10, 11, 80
Gravel
 gravel, 65, 66, 72, 77
Gravity
 gravity, 31, 38, 43, 44
Greenhouse
 greenhouse, 12, 13, 18, 19, 21, 22, 28, 36, 47, 48, 49, 50, 51, 55, 64, 66, 67, 74, 77
Himalayas, 65
Ice
 ice, 19, 23, 24, 25, 26, 27, 28, 29, 36, 42, 56, 58, 59, 66, 73, 77

Ice Age
  ice age
    Ice age, ix, 19, 20, 21, 23, 24, 25, 26, 27, 28, 29, 36, 37, 56, 59, 60, 67, 69, 72, 73, 74, 79
Impact site
  impact site, 22, 36, 38
Lava
  lava, 65
Manicouagan, 34
Mars, 16, 31, 34, 37, 40, 46, 55, 81
Methane
  methane, 13, 18, 48
Milankovitch, 23
Moisture cloud
  moisture cloud, 26, 28
Molten interior
  molten interior, 34
Mountains
  mountains, 10, 11, 19, 35, 36, 65, 66
New York, 79, 80, 81, 82, 83
orbit, 21, 31, 35, 37, 38, 39, 40, 43, 44, 45, 61, 64
Orbit
  orbit, 17, 66, 75, 76, 77
Oxygen
  oxygen, 50, 51, 52, 53, 60, 73
Rain
  rain, 8, 51, 52, 53, 54, 66
Rift
  rift, 55
Rivers
  rivers, 65
Rock
  rock, x, 10, 11, 16, 27, 32, 33, 34, 35, 36, 43, 55, 58, 59, 65, 66, 77
Russian, 13, 18, 48
Scotland, 65

Sedimentary
  sedimentary, x, 3, 10, 35, 36, 65, 66
Shockwave
  shockwave, 38, 40, 52, 54, 71, 72
Snow
  snow, 23, 24, 25, 26, 27, 28, 54, 56, 57, 58, 66, 69, 72, 73, 81
Solar Energy
  Solar energy
    solar energy, xi, 26, 53
South Africa, 34
Spitzbergen, 49
Submarine canyons
  submarine canyons, 58, 66
Sun
  sun, 13, 16, 17, 18, 19, 22, 23, 25, 26, 27, 28, 32, 34, 35, 37, 39, 42, 43, 44, 48, 49, 51, 56, 57, 64, 65, 66, 72, 74, 75, 83
Temperature
  temperature, x, xi, 11, 12, 15, 16, 18, 19, 20, 21, 22, 23, 24, 25, 27, 28, 29, 36, 44, 45, 46, 47, 48, 49, 50, 51, 52, 53, 57, 58, 59, 60, 61, 64, 66, 67, 71, 72, 73, 74, 75, 77
Tenitz Basin, 34, 35
Tunguska, 71
Vapour Canopy, 48
Wave
  wave, 3
Weather
  weather, 7, 15, 47, 61, 83
Wind
  wind, 3, 5, 7, 31, 35, 36
Window of Life, i, x, 36
Wobble
  wobble, 32
Woolly Mammoth, 20, 69, 72

www.ingramcontent.com/pod-product-compliance
Lightning Source LLC
Chambersburg PA
CBHW081507040426
42446CB00017B/3427